Understanding Writing Blocks

❧ *Understanding* *Writing Blocks*

Keith Hjortshoj
Cornell University

New York   Oxford
OXFORD UNIVERSITY PRESS
2001

Oxford University Press

Oxford   New York
Athens   Auckland   Bangkok   Bogotá   Buenos Aires   Calcutta
Cape Town   Chennai   Dar es Salaam   Delhi   Florence   Hong Kong   Istanbul
Karachi   Kuala Lumpur   Madrid   Melbourne   Mexico City   Mumbai
Nairobi   Paris   São Paulo   Shanghai   Singapore   Taipei   Tokyo   Toronto   Warsaw

and associated companies in
Berlin   Ibadan

Published by Oxford University Press, Inc.
198 Madison Avenue, New York, New York 10016
http://www.oup-usa.org

Oxford is a registered trademark of Oxford University Press

Library of Congress Cataloging-in-Publication Data

Hjortshoj, Keith.
        Understanding writing blocks / by Keith Hjortshoj.
            p. cm.
        Includes bibliographical references.
        ISBN 0-19-514136-9 (paper)
            1. English language—Rhetoric—Study and teaching.   2. Writer's block.   I. Title.

    PE1404.H58 2001
    8089.02'019—dc21   00-058034

9 8 7 6 5 4 3 2 1

Printed in the United States of America
on acid-free paper

Contents

Preface

When I began to work closely with blocked writers, around 1987, popular conceptions of "writer's block" led me to expect that I would discover a psychological or rhetorical syndrome that would account for most if not all of their problems. Through honest, thoughtful descriptions of their efforts to write, my students soon disillusioned me. Revealing diverse personalities, backgrounds, skills, and circumstances, these writers collectively refused to fit into a single category, and when my theories didn't fit their cases, they gently told me I was wrong.

Because these students led me to revise many tacit assumptions about writing and teaching, my gratitude extends well beyond their direct contributions to this book. To the extent that our exchanges got them moving toward the completion of their work, that account might be balanced. Through our discussions, however, I also began to recognize the ways in which teachers, advisors, and institutions are implicated in making writing difficult to varying degrees, and sometimes impossible. I became more aware of the directions in which we habitually push our students, with the assumption that they all need to put more effort into writing and reading, with higher standards and motivations. I realized that we are pushing some undergraduates and many graduate students in the wrong direction, into kinds of writing difficulty that seem mysterious only because they lie beyond the narrow conception that writing problems result from the lack of skill, effort, or motivation. Writing blocks confound us, I now suspect, because they often result from the goals, attitudes, and methods we encourage, and because they happen to the kinds of writers we want our students to become. Blocks happen to capable, highly motivated students and scholars like ourselves and our colleagues. Our own efforts to produce good writing are the factors that make progress slow and frustrating; and these same factors, when they become sufficiently entangled, bring progress to a halt.

I'm most indebted to my students for illuminating this largely hidden terrain where individual writers struggle to get their work done. I've enjoyed the freedom to explore these unconventional areas of writing and teaching with support from my colleagues in the Writing Workshop and the John S. Knight Institute for Writing in the Disciplines at Cornell University, where experimental, interdisciplinary views of writing have developed for more than thirty years. Most of the student writers mentioned in this book were enrolled in a course I developed with Barbara LeGendre and Joe Martin in the Writing Workshop, and this collaboration has added considerable depth to my understanding of the problems we try to solve.

Through his generous writing, teaching, and conversation, Peter Elbow has encouraged me to pay attention to the direction of our efforts in writing and teaching. Martha Hjortshoj, Bruce and Martha Fertman, and other teachers at the Alexander Alliance in Philadelphia have sharpened this sense of direction and allowed me to recognize the somatic dimensions of writing, as a kind of movement.

At Oxford University Press, Anthony English has given me wonderful encouragement and constructive advice since the moment he saw the proposal for this book. Thanks also to Benjamin Clark for skillfully steering it through copy editing and production.

Are Writing Blocks Real?

Writers may not be special—sensitive or talented
in any usual sense. They are simply engaged in sustained use of a language skill we all have. Their
"creations" come about through confident reliance
on stray impulses that will, with trust, find occa-
sional patterns that are satisfying.

WILLIAM STAFFORD

A PERSONAL PROBLEM?

When I began to work seriously on this book and looked for research literature on the subject, I had the alarming thought that perhaps everyone
who had tried to investigate writing blocks had become blocked and abandoned the task. How else could I explain the peculiar silence that surrounds
a malady that has such devastating effects on the lives of serious, capable
writers?

The few scholars who have completed studies of writing blocks also
found they were working almost in the dark. Zachary Leader began his literary discussion of blocks, in 1991, with the observation that "The first
point to make about *writer's block* is that relatively little has been written
about it. Although the phenomenon it means to designate can be found in
a variety of times and places, the actual term is of recent origin, and its air
of psychological substance and authority is largely an illusion." Consult-
ing the editors of the Oxford English Dictionary, Leader found that "Before the 1980's, a *writing block* meant simply 'a pad of paper'—'which is
much the same thing!' the senior editor added." The unabridged, interna-
tional edition of Webster's Dictionary still contains no entry for "writer's
block."

If writing blocks were essentially psychological disorders, as many people assume, we could expect that psychologists and psychiatrists would

1

have given considerable attention to this problem, identified its causes, and developed some standard treatments. Instead, as Robert Boice notes in his essay "Psychotherapies for Writing Blocks" (1985), scattered references to writing problems as psychological disorders have been "anecdotal—many are based entirely on the writer's self-treatment of a block—and almost all have been narrowly tied to a doctrinaire approach." Boice adds that there is "little clear sense of what writing blocks are or even of whether psychotherapists who employ, say, psychoanalytic versus cognitive approaches are treating the same problem as are writing specialists." To add to this confusion, psychologists and writing teachers often use the term *writer's block* interchangeably with the term *writer's anxiety*, on the unexamined assumption that emotions such as fear are the underlying causes of a writing block. Yet blocked writers are not always anxious writers. Some, in fact, are quite calm and have no noticeable fear of writing itself. In many other cases anxiety appears likely to be the *effect* of a block, not the cause.

Boice does cite one article that I take as the definitive statement on the insights on blocks offered by the field of psychology. In D. Upper's 1974 article in the *Journal of Applied Behavior Analysis*, the title "An Unsuccessful Self-Treatment of a Case of 'Writer's Block'" is followed by a blank page.

Although psychologists have little to say about these writing problems, the popular notion that they are psychological partly explains why writing teachers have ignored them as well. In his brief 1980 study of blocks among undergraduate writers, Mike Rose notes that we view weaknesses in student writing as the results of deficient ability, skill, or motivation. For these deficiencies, we offer "a bewildering panoply of treatments":

> But when the *capable* writer cannot write, we are puzzled and often resort to broad affective explanations, e.g., "He's afraid of evaluation," "She's too hard on herself." Significantly, the one possibly related topic that does appear in the research literature is "writing apprehension" or "writing anxiety"—again, affective. It is possible that this affective bent explains why writer's block has never been the object of the educator's scrutiny: it is perceived as a mysterious, amorphous emotional difficulty, not as a delimitable problem that can be analyzed and then remedied through instruction and tutorial programs.

Rose's 1984 monograph, called *Writer's Block*, remains a popular item in university libraries, but his work did not stimulate further research on the topic. The vast literature in the field of rhetoric and composition, which covers every other kind of writing problem imaginable, still contains few references to writing blocks. I will refer to some of these studies as they become relevant to following sections. For the purpose of understanding the nature of writing blocks, however, these individual articles do not add up to a body of literature, or even to a clearly discernible set of questions. A few universities have begun to offer general workshops or short courses for dissertation writers. Apart from a course I designed primarily for graduate students, however, I don't know of any formal instruction offered specifically for blocked writers. Supporting Rose's theory that this kind of writing difficulty is viewed as a "psychological" or emotional problem, psychological services on some campuses sponsor support groups in which blocked writers can discuss their problems. The Internet now contains several "chat groups" that serve similar purposes, along with commercial services that market "cures" for this affliction.

But there is another, related reason writing teachers seem to ignore blocks as serious writing problems. In higher education, most writing instruction is designed for college freshmen, to provide the skills and practice they will need for completing assignments at higher levels of the curriculum. Young, inexperienced writers rarely encounter serious blocks. For reasons that will become clear in following chapters, writing blocks are most common among advanced undergraduates, graduate students, scholars, and other professional writers who are not supposed to need help with writing and do not need the kinds of instruction offered in the typical composition class.

As a consequence, capable writers who feel hopelessly lost or immobilized in the process of writing usually conclude that these are personal problems, vaguely psychological, perhaps imaginary. Those who eventually come to me for help, in most cases, have been struggling with writing projects for months, even years, without openly admitting their difficulties. And when they do, the advice they receive from friends and teachers usually confirms their suspicion that the obstacles they encounter are "just in their head": more or less imaginary, "mental" blocks linked with perfectionism, insecurity, performance anxiety, or some other flaw in their personalities. *Just write!* friends tell them. *Just imagine you are speaking to a friend. Just talk into a tape recorder and write down what you said. Just schedule some time each day for writing, and stick with the schedule. Just relax!*

The "just" that launches this advice suggests that the barrier to productive writing is simply a kind of stubbornness, vanity, avoidance, or laziness. Writing would happen naturally, almost effortlessly, if these writers were not the kinds of people they happen to be, or if they did not have some mysterious little kink in their attitude toward writing. These messages are reinforced by most of the "self-help" books available for blocked writers. Following a series of rigid exercises in his book *Break Writer's Block Now!*, Jerrold Mundis concludes, with some ambivalence, that "Block is unreal. It stems almost entirely from Perfectionism, Fear, and the Baggage Train." In other words, if you were not such a fearful perfectionist with so much emotional baggage to haul around, you wouldn't have this problem. From a more explicitly psychological perspective, Victoria Nelson argues, in her book *On Writer's Block*, that recovery from this condition requires the resolution of deeply rooted conflicts between the creative "unconscious self" and the critical "conscious ego."

> Learning to protect oneself directly instead of indirectly through a creative block means, in the simplest terms, that one must learn to love oneself. For the *totum hominem*, this is the moral task of a lifetime. In writerly terms it can be addressed just as simply. To function as a writer, one must, above all, love and honor one's creative force, which can be pictured . . . as a kind of childlike spirit.

To become unblocked, therefore, one must become a more self-accepting, well-integrated individual. Nelson's argument might explain why writing teachers, untrained in psychotherapy, have so little advice to offer blocked writers, but it does not explain why productive, creative, successful writers have suffered from every kind of psychological disorder imaginable, including childish insecurities, self-loathing, and disintegrated personalities.

Victoria Nelson's book and a few others do offer some useful insights that I will mention farther on, but for college students, scholars, and many other professional writers these self-help books have another limitation. Most of the advice they offer concerns "expressive" writing such as fiction, poetry, or autobiography.

By contrast, most of the blocked writers I have known need to complete writing projects for their careers as students or as scholars. They have spent enormous amounts of time working on course papers, dissertations, research proposals, articles, or books, with little to show for their effort. As a consequence they have missed deadlines, failed courses, received "incompletes," or taken leaves of absence. Some had already lost fellowship support, were facing threats of expulsion, or were in danger of failing tenure or promotion reviews in institutions where "publish or perish" is a ruthless imperative. To varying degrees these writers have been depressed, anxious, and discouraged. Most of them had very high standards for writing, were afraid of failure, and had fallen into some pattern of avoidance. To a great extent, however, these emotional and behavioral conditions were the effects of their difficulties with writing, not the causes.

These writers who found help with writing blocks represent a very small proportion of those who need help. In a 1992 interview in *Writing on the Edge*, Peter Elbow said "scratch an academic and you'll find someone who's in trouble with writing," and this is only a slight exaggeration. At my own university alone, hundreds of people who must write and are not supposed to need help with writing have trouble, sometimes desperate trouble, nonetheless. Because writing is the main form of currency in higher education and largely determines one's success or failure, severe difficulties with writing are probably most common in universities. For people who fail to complete writing projects, however, comparably severe consequences apply in journalism, business, law, and many other professions that require extensive writing.

These are the kinds of writers I have most in mind as the audience for this book, which concerns types of writing problems that are extremely common but largely hidden, politely ignored, and mystified. For the people who experience serious writing blocks, these problems are intensely real. Although writing blocks fall outside the categories of problems addressed by psychologists and writing teachers, if you encounter blocks I want to assure you that these problems have specific causes, characteristics, and solutions.

WHAT BLOCKS ARE NOT

Before I explain what writing blocks are, I should explain what they are not, and why so much confusion and mystery surrounds these problems.

Although the term "writer's block" is very recent, it resembles early medical terms, such as "the vapors," used to describe a wide range of loosely related symptoms as the effects of a single mysterious or fictitious cause. "Writer's block" probably derives from the broader term "mental block," used to explain all sorts of obstacles, lapses, and aversions—when our minds go blank unexpectedly, when our memories fail us, or when we can't face something. "Mental block" is simply a way of describing something we can't explain.

In popular usage, therefore, the term "writer's block" is a false category. People use this term to account for almost any difficulty, delay, or failure to write that seems mysterious, as a label for problems they can't explain or didn't anticipate. Students have told me they had "writer's block" because they couldn't immediately think of a topic for a paper due the next day, or because they stared at the computer screen for a few minutes, waiting for inspiration. *Why can't I think of anything to say? How did I get stuck in the middle of this project? Why am I still rewriting this sentence? Why is Helen still working on that article that was due five months ago? Why did George fail to complete his dissertation? Why did Charlotte abandon work on that novel she was writing? Why did Herman Melville, E. M. Forster, Dashiell Hammett, and many other famous authors stop producing books?*

"Writer's block" provides a readily available answer to these questions, without really answering them at all. People run into trouble in the writing process, fail to complete projects, or stop writing altogether for many reasons, including lack of experience, unrealistic expectations, loss of interest and motivation, procrastination, and the decision to do something else with their time. If "writer's block" refers to the effects of all of these conditions, along with obscure psychological disorders, the term simply represents our confusion about a realm of human activity that is extremely difficult to understand. This loose collection of meanings explains why the kinds of writing problems we call "blocks" remain undefined, unstudied, and unresolved. If these problems have diverse, unrelated causes, the term blurs distinctions and has no particular meaning.

To give the term real meaning and clarity, I'll eliminate some of its meanings in popular usage, and briefly explain why I'm doing so.

• *A delay in the process of writing is not in itself a writing block.* In the next two chapters I'll explain more fully why delays of varying lengths are normal, necessary features of writing, even though they can become frustrating.

• *Lack of inspiration is not a writing block.* If you feel that you have nothing to say at the moment, perhaps you don't have anything to say. A feeling of muteness can result from a writing block, but we spend most of our time without feeling inspired to write, and during that time we are not necessarily blocked from writing.

• For similar reasons, *lack of motivation is not in itself a writing block*, though it can result from one. If you genuinely have no reason to write something, are not willing to spend the time and effort, you are simply unmotivated, not blocked. Hundreds of thousands of people have thought about writing novels, perhaps started to write one, and abandoned the task. The great majority of these people are not sufficiently motivated to complete such a demanding project. "Writer's block" is not preventing them from writing.

• Some of these people also lacked the ability, knowledge, or experience to complete the task, but *incapability is not a writing block.* If someone asked me to write an article on quantum mechanics or a book on Mozart, I would fail, unless I first spent a long time becoming capable of writing about these subjects. This failure would not result from a writing block.

- *Writing blocks are not reliably linked with personality types or mental conditions.* Some types of people, such as perfectionists, are perhaps susceptible to writing blocks. Depression complicates and can result from writing difficulties. But it is often impossible to determine whether these conditions are causes or effects, and the people who have come to me for help have no consistent characteristics. Individuals among them have been light-hearted or gloomy, orderly or messy, anxious or calm, outgoing or shy. As I mentioned above, successful, prolific writers also represent every type of person, including every kind of mental disorder, so particular psychological factors cannot reliably cause writing blocks.

- *Writing blocks rarely affect all writing.* Writers become blocked while they are working on specific types of writing or specific tasks. They can usually complete other kinds of writing without much difficulty. Someone who is struggling with a dissertation, for example, might continue to write letters, reports, diary entries, or even articles for publication without encountering the same kinds of obstacles.

- *Writing blocks occur at particular places in the writing process.* For this reason blocked writers might produce large amounts of writing up to that point in the writing process, but cannot move beyond it. As a consequence, the idea that blocked writers simply stare at the blank page, unable to find anything to say, is a fiction.

I have listed these exclusions and misconceptions because they often lead writers to imagine that they "have writer's block" when they do not, and because these misconceptions lead writers of all kinds to false conclusions about the real difficulties they experience. Writers who are mired in a project often feel that they must reorganize their lives, resolve emotional problems, or complete extensive therapy in order to make progress. Even if these are worthwhile endeavors, progress with writing does not depend upon them. Occasionally, people who appear to be struggling with writing blocks have simply lost interest in their work, want to do something else with their time, and haven't yet admitted this to themselves. The solution for this kind of "block" is to stop trying to write something you do not really care about and take an honest assessment of what you want to do with that time.

A misconception about "writer's block" can also induce one. Alison, a college junior, once came to my office because she could not finish papers in an advanced anthropology course. When I asked Alison what she believed the problem was, she said that she thought she had "writer's block" caused by a learning disability. Because Alison was having trouble revising an unsuccessful draft of a complex paper, her friend, who was dyslexic, suggested that Alison should take a learning disability test, which identified some kind of minor pattern. Having found the "cause" of her difficulty, Alison gave up on the revision and also failed to write the next paper for the course.

Looking at the first draft she had written, however, I discovered that before she surrendered to "writer's block" Alison had made excellent handwritten plans for revision. Because this was the most complex assignment she had received, and she had never thoroughly revised a paper in the past, she had felt her writing was a hopeless mess and became discouraged. Curing Alison's "writer's block" required about twenty minutes of my time. I simply told her that she did not have a writing block, that a learning disability was not the cause of her problems with these papers, that extensive revision is a completely normal part of writing a complex paper, and that she should follow her own plans for revision.

If the term "writer's block" represents a false, misleading category of writing problems that blurs distinctions and causes more problems than it explains, perhaps we should abandon the term altogether, and call its assorted referents by other, more precise names.

This is why I have put "writer's block" in quotation marks thus far and will not use the term to describe the problems I define below. In part, I avoid the term because it has a clinical ring to it that suggests a psychological disorder, like claustrophobia or vertigo.

I will continue to refer to *writing blocks*, however, because the word "block" does accurately describe the almost physical obstacles that writers encounter. And these blocks are extreme cases of a larger category of writing difficulties that I will call *interference* with movement through the writing process, and with our ability to write. Because all serious writers experience at least minor forms of interference in the process of writing, understanding the nature of writing blocks can be useful to everyone who writes extensively.

THOUGHT AND MOVEMENT

When I explained in the previous section what writing blocks are not, I also defined blocked writers, by exclusion, as *capable, motivated writers who seem incapable of completing certain kinds of writing projects.* These people have clear reasons for writing, and the task at hand is often crucial to their careers. They also have plenty of ideas and information to write about (often too many ideas, and too much information). Blocked writers, furthermore, are rarely perceived to be incompetent, weak writers. Their readers, friends, teachers, and supervisors usually expect them to write well without much difficulty, often on the basis of past performance. And in most cases they can write without trouble in other circumstances, or in some phases of the writing process. This is why advice such as *Just write!* is of little help. They *can* just write in other contexts, even about the task that gives them so much difficulty. But in that task they continually reach an impasse.

There lies the mystery of a writing block: in the fact that we can't explain this problem in conventional terms of ability, knowledge, or motivation. Somewhere in the process of doing something they want and need to do, and are fully capable of doing, these writers run into trouble they shouldn't have.

I've also described this trouble, this block, as an almost physical obstacle that writers can't move beyond, and I arrived at this description through the language writers use to explain what they experience. When referring to their struggles, these writers frequently say that they feel *immobilized, motionless, stuck, stranded, mired, derailed, disengaged, disembodied, paralyzed,* or *numb.* "I'm just not getting anywhere," they say, or, "I feel like I'm going around in circles." One graduate student told me, "I feel like I'm standing on something I'm trying to lift."

In other words, *they describe these writing problems in the language of movement and physical sensation,* typically as a lack of movement and sensation, in spite of great effort. Their descriptions often recall those dreams in which we are trying desperately to run or to swim but can't get anywhere, because our limbs won't function properly.

If I viewed writing entirely as a mental activity I would consider this language of movement and physical experience to be metaphorical. But the notion that writing is purely mental is what leads us to the conclusion that a writing block is an imaginary condition, "just in the writer's head"—a conclusion that is not at all helpful. Writing cannot be purely mental because *thinking, in itself, does not produce writing.* As all blocked writers know entirely too well, thinking *about* writing also does not produce writing. Yet writing is obviously not just physical movement either. In theory, perhaps, an infinite number of monkeys with typewriters would eventually produce *Hamlet,* but their random pokes at the keyboard would not be writing. Language skills, thoughts, and intentions must direct this physical movement. Like almost everything else that we do, writing is both mental and physical. And if these dimensions of the self in the world are not co-ordinated, writing will not happen.

When I became interested in writing blocks, I had also become alert to this "interface" (as people in the computer industry would call it) because I was involved in a kind of movement study called the Alexander Technique. A contemporary of John Dewey, George Bernard Shaw, and Aldous Huxely (who were among his students), F. M. Alexander was an Australian actor who lost his voice during performances. Doctors could not solve the problem, and because the use of his voice was essential to his career, Alexander was forced to investigate the cause of this affliction on his own. Over several years, his investigations led to deeper, more general understandings of the principles underlying coordinated movement—discoveries Alexander described in a book called *The Use of the Self.* The teaching methods he later developed are best known among performers—musicians, actors, and dancers—but people study the Alexander Technique to become more coordinated and comfortable in all kinds of movement.

Although the physical discomforts of writing (sitting for long periods before a computer screen, for example) can complicate writing difficulties, I was most interested in Alexander's realization that the cause and the solution for his problem were, as he said, "psycho-physical": rooted in stimulus/response patterns that were at once mental and physical. Early in his investigations Alexander recognized that his loss of voice resulted from something he was *doing* when he spoke on stage, and he then figured out (from watching himself in mirrors) what that something was. Just as he spoke he pushed his head back and down, thus compressing his spine and larynx. This habitual movement probably began as an *idea* that this was the right way to project one's voice, and when he realized it was the wrong thing to do Alexander imagined that the problem was virtually solved.

But it was not, for two reasons. First, abandoning an established, habitual pattern of movement was much harder than he had expected. At the last instant he involuntarily fell into that same pattern of compression, even when he thought he was avoiding it. Breaking this habit was also complicated by his misconceptions about the way his head and neck really worked, which prevented him from knowing and altering what he was actually doing. "All the damn fools in the world," he later observed, "believe they are actually doing what they think they are doing." Ineffective, uncoordinated ways of doing things are linked with mistaken, unexamined assumptions about structure and movement that make these ways of doing things "feel right" in the moment, even when we know intellectually that they get us into trouble.

Like other activities, writing is a kind of embodied movement, more or less coordinated by ideas about what we are and should be doing. The people who came to me for help because they had failed to complete writing projects had not been sitting motionless in front of a blank page all those weeks or months, and their minds were not blank either. They had been thinking about their writing, sometimes obsessively, and they had been doing things, including things they considered to be writing. Blocked writers are often very industrious, and work on their projects for several hours each day. Activities related to their work included reading, extensive notetaking, making schedules, gathering information, analyzing data, outlining, composing portions of drafts, rewriting, and editing sentences. In other words, they were often engaged in the routine procedures productive writers use to get work done.

I want to emphasize that there is nothing inherently wrong with any of these procedures. Reading and other kinds of investigation are essential to almost all academic work and to most kinds of journalism, reports, and other professional writing. Outlines and other plans can be useful. Most good writers extensively revise and carefully edit drafts.

Blocked writers simply do these things at the wrong times or in the wrong proportions, sometimes for the wrong reasons. As a consequence, their movements within the writing process do not lead to its completion. At crucial moments that we can usually identify, they do something that seems like the right thing to do, or that they can't resist doing. At that moment, movement through the writing process stops or turns in an unproductive (often repetitive) direction. While composing sentences, perhaps, they stop to read, to reconsider what they just said, or to edit. When they find themselves departing from an outline, they stop to make a new one. Or when they feel they are gathering momentum in a certain direction, they take a break and lose momentum.

These stimulus/response patterns, in particular moments, are writing blocks. And these are very real things blocked writers do, in their minds and in their bodies. In turn, altering what is done in these moments resolves writing blocks. Sometimes this change comes about easily, in a matter of hours. Sometimes, unpredictably, the pattern is deeply rooted and persists for months, even years.

BLOCKS ARE REAL WRITING PROBLEMS

Why do individuals fall into these specific patterns?

Efforts to answer this question can easily lead us into the depths of a writer's personality, emotional development, and past experience. Sometimes these explorations are useful, and sometimes they are not. Occasionally, conversations about writing problems reveal that the difficulty is linked with a certain experience or relationship—typically a bad experience, bad advice, an unreasonably demanding teacher or parent, or an unrealistic goal. The identification of this faulty connection can help to make writing easier, more pleasurable, and more productive. Untangling a writing problem can also stimulate changes in other important dimensions of life.

But I am a professional writing teacher, not a psychotherapist. In my area of expertise, I'm interested in the ways in which people use language in a full sense that includes not only what they write but also their ideas about writing, their conceptions of themselves as writers, and their methods. Like my teaching, this book will remain moored to the activity of writing itself as a dimension of our lives that we can observe, understand, and alter. And while the investigation of this domain will carry us briefly into other realms, including emotional ones, we will not stray far from their direct relation to our efforts to get writing done.

I mention this because the writers I teach are often anxious, frustrated, and discouraged—emotionally distressed. Their struggles to complete projects undermine their composure, lead them to question their ability, and sometimes disrupt other parts of their lives. Some of you are probably reading this book with feelings of disturbance and confusion about writing. It would be easy for us to dwell on the turmoil that frequently surrounds a writing block, and to feel that we must restore order and calm before we can make progress.

While I accept and do not try to suppress these implications of writing problems, I've learned from experience not to dwell on them, or to feel that I need to resolve them. Instead, I want to know as much as possible about the writing itself:

What kind of writing are you trying to do?

How do you approach this task?

At what point, exactly, does progress end?

What do you do up to that point?

When you reach it, what do you do next, and why?

Answers to these questions allow us to understand Alison's brief episode of "writer's block" quite easily. Although her feelings about this problem were strong and real, dwelling on these responses would not have removed the obstacle. Instead, we quickly reached an understanding and solution through an analysis of the ideas and circumstances that surrounded her inability to complete her papers:

While working on her first complex college paper, which she expected to complete in one draft, Alison ran into difficulty when she realized the draft needed revision. The idea that she had a learning disability, combined with misconceptions of the writing process, then provided a false explanation for her struggles and led her to stop writing at that point in the process. Until she altered her ideas about the problem and acted upon that change, she could not move beyond the obstacle. Because Alison had only recently adopted these ideas about her writing, did not entirely believe them, and was happy to alter them, she surmounted the block almost immediately. If she had not sought and found help so quickly, subsequent failures might have supported her notion that she was a disabled writer, and the problem would have become increasingly difficult to resolve.

All writing blocks occur somewhere within the process of writing. And while teachers and scholars in my profession seem to ignore writing blocks per se, they do have useful things to tell us about what writing actually is, what people are doing in the process, and how finished writing comes about. Because blocks often result from misconceptions—mismappings—of the writing process, we should first draw an accurate map of this terrain that writers move through.

Product and Process

Performance, in which the whole fate and terror
rests, is another matter.

JAMES AGEE

THE VALUE OF PRIVACY

On the shelf in my office is a book with a title that sends a chill down my
spine when I notice it, especially when I'm writing. It is *The Reader Over
Your Shoulder*, by Robert Graves and Alan Hodge. This old-
fashioned British handbook for writers, first published in 1943, views writing as a form of public behavior that must be governed by strict rules of
propriety and order. Graves and Hodge begin with essays on the history,
corruption, and abuse of the English language and then offer about forty
principles devoted to the resurrection of literary virtue. "All ideas should
be expressed concisely, but without discourteous abruptness," these principles warn, and "Even when the natural order of words is modified for
the sake of emphasis, a sentence must not read unnaturally." Having de-
livered these intricate prescriptions for Good Writing, Graves and Hodge
demonstrate just how hazardous the enterprise can be by applying their
standards to the published work of Bertrand Russell, George Bernard Shaw,
T. S. Eliot, and a dozen other luminaries of their time. All of these famous
writers committed several infractions—such as MISPLACED WORDS,
UNFULFILLED PROMISES, FAULTY CONNEXIONS, AND MIS-
PUNCTUATION—in each paragraph under scrutiny.

The Reader Over Your Shoulder leads us to the conclusion that it is virtually impossible to use written English without abusing the language and
making fools of ourselves in public. *Watch out! Keep all of these rules in
mind at every moment. Critical readers are waiting for you to make a false
move. You can never be good enough!*

Why do I keep this nagging nanny on my shelf? Once I turned the spine to the wall, to remind myself that the title was false. In reality there was no reader looking over my shoulder. I was completely free to write for readers who remained imaginary, without feeling that they were already breathing down my neck, scrutinizing every sentence I produced. I didn't want real readers anywhere near me.

For this reason, however, *The Reader Over Your Shoulder* also reminds me of Paul, a courageous student who taught me just how devastating such readers can be when they *are* real.

A junior in college at the time, Paul seemed like a typical undergraduate in my upper-level writing class. He had turned in, on time, two more or less average papers for the class, and I was surprised when he came to my office one day to apologize for their poor quality. Although he had overcome a terrible writing block in his first year of college, he explained, writing was still an extremely stressful, laborious process. He just wanted me to know that although he was a bad writer, he was working hard and trying to improve.

I knew very little about writing blocks then, and because Paul seemed to want to talk about the problem, I asked him why writing had been so difficult. I also asked why he thought he was a bad writer.

His father, Paul explained, was a professional writer who wanted to help his son meet his own high standards. Even when Paul was in elementary school his father had insisted on reading, criticizing, and correcting drafts of everything he wrote before teachers saw his work, and this criticism was so thorough that Paul soon concluded that he hadn't inherited a shred of his father's talent. Paul got decent grades, of course, but he felt that his father's help only masked his incompetence. Over the years, his writing got worse, not better. As assignments became more complex, he needed increasing amounts of assistance, and by the time he graduated from high school Paul dreaded writing anything because he knew he would have to show it to his father, and knew it would be terrible. His whole high school record, he said, fraudulently concealed his inability to write. His father had completely rewritten all of his college application essays, to the extent that Paul believed that they represented his father's qualifications, not his own.

When he entered college, therefore, the fraud would be exposed. Everything Paul wrote would immediately reveal his lack of ability, especially to English teachers. At the beginning of his freshman year, Paul told me, he couldn't complete even a paragraph without feeling so angry and incompetent that he crumpled the page, threw it away, and started a new draft that was equally bad. He was completely, hopelessly blocked.

Describing a very similar problem in his psychoanalytic case study of a blocked writer, in the *Journal of Advanced Composition*, Nick Tingle suggests that this kind of block results from such deeply rooted emotional disorders that there are no practical solutions. Tingle refers to an undergraduate whose mother was a literature professor, her sister a successful novelist. Feeling unable to meet these high standards, the student plagiarized her papers to avoid revealing that she "could not write." Tingle concludes that this was a purely "psychological" writing disorder:

> This student's difficulty with writing did not seem to me then and does not seem to me now explicable in terms of theories of cognition. No amount of instruction in writing as problem solving or writing as a process was going to improve this student's performance, not because her powers of cognition were weak but because of her psychological relation to writing.

Yet Paul *had* found ways of using the writing process that helped to solve his problem, without help from writing teachers or from psychotherapists.

"But you *do* finish papers," I said to him. "And you're a junior now, still in school. You even *chose* to take my course. What on earth did you do?"

With a wary smile, Paul said, "If you look closely at my papers you'll always find some little flaw—a dot of ink maybe, or a little tear, usually down in the corner or on the back."

I looked at one of his papers and soon found the flaws he described. There was a dot of ink at the bottom of one page, a small corner torn from another. "I don't understand," I confessed. "How does this help you write?"

Paul explained that he had dropped his freshman writing course in his first semester because he couldn't complete any of the papers. In his second semester he took another required writing class, couldn't do the first assignment, and made up some excuse. As the deadline for the second paper approached, he was still struggling to write paragraphs on a notepad and throwing pages away by the dozen when he realized he was going to fail and would have to leave school in shame. In desperation, then, he decided it was better to turn in horrible writing than none at all, so he fished one of his unfinished paragraphs out of the wastebasket, smoothed out the paper, and tried to continue. He noticed that writing seemed a little easier on this ruined paper he had already thrown away and resurrected; crumpled paper was more appropriate, he felt, for the awkward sentences he was writing. When he had filled that page with more sentences, therefore, he wadded up a clean sheet and smoothed it out before he began to write on it, and later, when he began to produce a second draft, he continued to ruin pages before he wrote on them.

These revisions consumed many hours over several days, and the essay was late, but at least he got it finished. The teacher's criticism wasn't as harsh as he had expected; perhaps he could pass the course after all. For the next assignment, Paul started out writing on crumpled paper and invented a rule that however bad the writing seemed, he was not allowed to throw it away. In successive drafts he found that he could do less damage to the pages—just fold them in half or scribble on the back. Obviously he couldn't turn in papers that looked like they had been through the laundry. But even on the typed copy he needed to do something to mar the unspoiled surface that told him his writing had to be good, because he genuinely felt that his writing was never good enough. He passed his writing seminar with a C, and in following semesters he used these methods whenever he had to write. He had even stopped avoiding courses that required papers and essay exams.

"I know this is weird," he said self-consciously, "and it still takes me forever to produce rough papers. But at least I get them done. I'm still here."

What Paul had to recover from was a writer's worst nightmare: a critical reader he admired, trusted, and wanted very much to please who was *actually* looking over his shoulder, making free movement through the writing process impossible, reminding him of his incompetence, and leading him to the conclusion that he had no writing ability of his own. What Paul actually experienced, in the form of "help" with his writing, is what we are often encouraged to imagine for the purpose of writing well: that writing is at every moment a public performance for critical readers who maintain standards we cannot meet, according to rules we never learned or cannot follow. If we take this advice to heart, the process of writing becomes, at every step, movement into a minefield of potential errors and humiliations.

STAGE FRIGHT IN REHEARSAL

We can easily understand why Paul felt that a critical reader was looking over his shoulder. One was. But how do the rest of us get into this frame of mind, in which we imagine that the process is already the performance—that the audience is already reading, evaluating, every word? This common type of interference with our ability resembles performance anxiety, but "stage fright" usually occurs when performers are actually on stage, before a real audience, not when they are rehearsing in the privacy of a studio. Musicians rarely confuse practice with performance, and they know that they can't expect to perform beautifully without rehearsal. Why are writers so vulnerable to the idea that what they are saying at the moment is already reaching the reader, and represents the finished product?

Books such as *The Reader Over Your Shoulder* offer one answer to this question. In the United States as in England, schools have traditionally taught writing as a form of public behavior and have emphasized the qualities of finished products, not the process through which writing comes about. Process and product are conflated even in the word "writing," which can refer either to the activity ("I'm writing a paper") or to the object, the completed text ("His writing lacks organization"). Throughout high school and college, most of us wrote almost entirely for courses and teachers, and almost all of this work was graded. While we are writing, therefore, it is easy to imagine the risk of errors, misunderstandings, and criticism later on.

For the same reason, *disassociation* with performance usually makes writing easier. Ruined paper was easier for Paul to write on because it could not be the page anyone else would read. When I ask students to write in class and assure them that no one will read what they say, they visibly relax into the task and write very quickly. When I tell them they will turn in their writing or show it to classmates, they work more slowly and cautiously, frequently pausing to consider what they are saying and how it will sound. This is why we can write so quickly and comfortably in a private diary. I once knew a young poet who wore a hideous plastic shower cap when she worked on her poems to remind herself that she was alone, that she could do or say anything—that appearances did not yet matter.

Another reason for confusion between product and process lies in the powerful connections between writing and speech. Speech is prior to writing both historically and developmentally. While the ability to speak to one another is almost synonymous with our humanity, the first written languages developed only about six thousand years ago, and until the nineteenth century literacy remained an extraordinary skill. We also begin to process spoken language almost at birth (recent research observed alertness to sentence structure at the age of 7 months!), and can converse with reasonable fluency before we even begin to learn how to read and write. Because the written language we learned is the symbolic representation of spoken language, we can easily think of writing as "speaking on paper," or as a record of speech.

And in some respects it is. Connection with the sounds and rhythms of speech is what gives writing "voice" and fluency, both for writers and for readers. We write and read with what Eudora Welty (in *One Writer's Be-*

ginnings) called her "reader-voice": the vocal qualities of the language itself, resonating in our minds and on the page.

Ever since I was first read to, then started reading to myself, there has never been a line that I didn't hear. As my eyes followed the sentence, a voice was saying it silently to me. It isn't my mother's voice, or the voice of any person I can identify, certainly not my own. It is human, but inward, and it is inwardly that I listen to it. It is to me the voice of the story or poem itself. The cadence, whatever it is that asks you to believe, the feeling that resides in the printed word, reaches me through the reader-voice. I have supposed, but never found out, that this is the case with all readers—to read as listeners—and with all writers, to write as listeners. It may be part of the desire to write. The sound of what falls on the page begins the process of testing it for truth, for me. . . .

My own words, when I am at work on a story, I hear too as they go, in the same voice that I hear when I read in books. When I write and the sound of it comes back to my ears, then I act to make my changes. I have always trusted this voice.

In turn, when we do not listen to that "reader-voice," or do not trust it, writing loses its essential connection with speech and sounds mechanically assembled.

Yet writing differs from speech in some equally fundamental ways, directly relevant to writing difficulties. In conversation, spoken language reaches the audience immediately. In this respect, speech is performance and cannot be revised, as Roland Barthes observed in *Image-Music-Text*:

> Speech is irreversible: a word cannot be *retracted*, except precisely by saying that one retracts it. To cross out is here to add: if I want to erase what I have just said, I cannot do it without showing the eraser itself (I must say: *'or rather . . .' 'I expressed myself badly . . .'*); paradoxically, it is ephemeral speech which is indelible, not monumental writing. All that one can do in the case of a spoken utterance is to tack on another utterance.

One might expect, then, that "stage fright" would afflict speakers more than writers, but in conversation we can usually compose sentences spontaneously and almost continuously, much as jazz musicians compose music as they perform it. Although we usually can't rehearse and revise conversational speech, language flows without much interruption because the audience is there with us, listening and responding. We can use gestures and expressions to embellish what we say, and the listeners' responses help us adapt what we are saying to the information they provide about their expectations. When you make a statement in conversation, if the listener immediately scowls or looks perplexed you can take that response into account while you speak. You know that you need to support that statement or clarify it. Speaking is usually a highly interactive, intersubjective, embodied activity. What we are doing at the time is connected with what we are saying. In literary and theatrical terms, the presence of a responsive audience makes it easier to assemble an effective *persona*: the kind of person we represent ourselves to be for a particular occasion.

Electronic communication helps to illustrate why the construction of persona can be more difficult in writing. A telephone-answering machine simulates the problem of writing, because it forces us to speak to people who are not there as though they *were* there. Many of us have trouble speaking naturally and spontaneously in this situation. We have to think about what we are going to say and speak haltingly, as though we were waiting for replies: . . . *So . . . call me back when you get a chance . . . okay? . . . well . . . I guess that's all . . . ah . . . so long. . . .* Before I got used to these devices, when I connected with an answering machine I really wanted to hang up the phone, compose a message, and call back. I began to worry about the way my voice would sound on the tape, which would capture my speech much as a written message is captured on paper. I therefore became self-conscious about speaking, which began to seem like a performance. Most of us would have even more difficulty speaking spontaneously, calmly, and coherently into a radio microphone or a television camera to large audiences of people we don't know and can't see, and who don't respond.

In writing, the act of utterance and the act of communication (or performance) are separated both in time and in space. And this separation represents both the great disadvantage and the great advantage of writing— the cause of its difficulty and the source of its power. In speech we need most of all to be aware of ourselves and of others in the moment. When we write, almost everything in our immediate environment is a potential distraction from a work of the imagination that can seem disembodied. Walter Ong captured this paradox in his book *Orality and Literacy*:

> I am writing a book that I hope will be read by hundreds of thousands of people, so I must be isolated from everyone. While writing the present book, I have left word that I am "out" for hours and days—so that no one, including persons who will presumably read the book, can interrupt my solitude.

For this reason, extremely active, extroverted people who thrive on interaction often find writing especially unsettling as a medium of communication. Sitting still for long periods alone without immediate response from an audience makes them feel cut off from direct communication, and restless.

On the other hand, writing should be an ideal medium for introverts who feel rushed and unprepared to speak in conversation. These people should welcome the time and solitude they need to compose their thoughts before they actually say something—to rehearse before they go on stage. This delay between utterance and reception is what led the poet William Stafford to call writing "one of the great, free human activities." In that time, we are free to say anything that occurs to us in complete privacy, without fear of misunderstanding, humiliation, or criticism. Unlike speech, what we say in writing can be reconsidered, altered, thrown away, rewritten, and polished. Until we choose to release this work to the reader, we can take it back, and unless we reveal these procedures, no one will ever know how the product actually came about. The best writing will sound as though it just came out that way, in a continuous, fluent stream.

Like all good performance, however, good writing erases its own history and, as Barthes would say, conceals the eraser. In the performance of a fine pianist we shouldn't sense all of the effort, error, and alteration that occurred in the privacy of rehearsal. The performance should create an illusion of ease, as though the performer could just sit down and play beautifully without difficulty.

But this illusion of ease in the best work we read can blur the difference between performance and rehearsal and lead writers to feel that they should be able to perform beautifully throughout the process, at every utterance. To enjoy the great benefits of writing over speech, we need to realize in the moment, while we are writing, that what we are saying is not yet communication. We need to realize, in other words, that while we are doing it writing is a process, not a product.

WHAT ARE YOU ACTUALLY DOING?

I emphasize this distinction because all of our real difficulties with writing occur in the process, yet in that process most of our anxieties, doubts, and hopes focus on the reception of a product that does not yet exist: *Will I get this finished on time? Will it be good enough? What will readers think of it? Will it sound stupid? Will they understand it? Will they agree with me? Will this ever get published? Will the committee approve it? Will it get a good grade?*

These anticipations distract our attention from what we are actually doing and disrupt the coordination of language and thought. Imagining the outcome largely creates the sense that writing is a disembodied activity—something that happens only in the mind and imagination. Sitting, in itself, does not cause us to lose awareness that we are there in our bodies, doing something in particular in time and space, for we can do other quiet things—knitting, or reading—without feeling disembodied.

We can easily become lost in time and space while writing because when it is viewed as a whole process that includes the reader, writing is a relativistic medium. In other words, what I am writing now is connected with what you eventually read, but in different reference frames. I am sitting here in my office at a particular time, working on page 24 of this manuscript. You are reading the words I write, so I am communicating something to you. While I am writing, however, you are not yet reading, and the specific text you read does not yet exist in the form you have. To write I must at least vaguely imagine a reader, and while you are reading you can imagine me writing what you read, but neither vision is very reliable. I don't really know how this writing will strike you, and while I must have a sense of audience in mind, to enjoy the freedom of writing I also need to remember that you remain a figment of my imagination—one whose responses I can't control. In turn, you are probably not on page 24, and although you might assume that I wrote this passage before the sections and chapters that follow, I did not. I'm inserting these paragraphs into a full draft of the book, which will no doubt change in other ways before you read it. I might decide to take this passage out again, so at the moment I can't be sure that it will ever reach you, my imagined reader. Yet the decisions I make will directly affect the outcome.

If we are actually doing things when we write, what are we doing? What is this "psychophysical" process we move through? Where does it start, what direction does it take, and where does it end? Writers who experience blocks need most of all to consider these questions, because something they are doing along the way prevents them from reaching the end.

Until the 1970s, composition teachers and textbooks advocated a tidy sequence of procedures for producing tidy essays. *Choose a topic. Make an outline. Follow the outline while writing the paper. Check your work to make sure it is clear and correct.* Many American schools still prescribe these linear methods, along with formulas for organization such as the "five-paragraph theme" or the "keyhole essay."

The resulting emphasis on neatness, organization, and correctness in the English class conflicted sharply with popular images of writers at work: hunched over their typewriters, red-eyed and disheveled, wrestling with their demons and muses in a litter of coffee cups (or liquor bottles) and crumpled drafts. Most of us grew up with these contradictory images of the way Good Writing comes about. On the one hand, the process of writing is largely a matter of following rules and instructions for the assembly of a certain kind of product—the shortest route to a known destination. On the other hand, writing is a messy and often frustrating journey into the unknown, guided by imagination. "You go into a book," James Baldwin said, "and you're in the dark, really. You go in with a certain fear and trembling. You know one thing. You know you will not be the same person when this journey is over."

To some extent this contradiction results from real variations among methods, attitudes, and types of writing. Novelists do not necessarily share Baldwin's approach. "Here is a useful rule for beginning," John Irving said. "Know the story—as much of the story as you can possibly know, if not the whole story—before you commit yourself to the first paragraph." And methods used for writing novels are not necessarily appropriate for writing business reports, dissertations in the field of history, scientific articles, or papers for a sociology class. Joan Didion was at least partly right when she observed that "The element of discovery takes place, in nonfiction, not during the writing but in the research. This makes writing a piece very tedious. You already know what it's about." Writers are often afflicted by the suspicion that there is a Right Way to proceed that they are not following, but successful writers, even within a single genre, have many ways of getting through the process. To the extent that it gets the job done, one method is as good as another.

When scholars began to investigate what writers were actually doing, however, they found that they were rarely, if ever, following a purely linear series of "stages" like those prescribed in composition textbooks. In her study of twelfth graders and professional writers, in 1971, Janet Emig learned that although they used very different methods, neither group extensively used or followed outlines. All of the sixteen professional writers in her study engaged in "planning" of various kinds, but their plans changed throughout the process and only four constructed formal outlines. When Emig asked twenty-five honors English students to save all of the written material they produced in completing 109 essays for their class, only 40 of these essays included written plans of any sort, and only 9 included formal outlines. Evaluations of the finished papers, by a panel of English teachers, revealed no correlation between the use of outlines, either formal or informal, and the quality or organization of the finished product.

Unlike the professional writers in Emig's study, who revised drafts extensively, these high school students rarely rewrote their first drafts. How could they produce coherent papers without plans or revisions? Emig found that the most successful writers were inclined to "compose aloud": rehearsing, reading, and generally voicing what they were writing while they composed.

Other studies confirmed that most writers are neither plodding through a series of distinct procedures nor "just writing": engaged in a single kind of activity. "When composition texts describe writing as a series of tidy sequential steps," Linda Flower and John Hayes observed in a 1980 article called "The Dynamics of Composing,"

> the role of the writer is like that of a cook baking a cake or a CPA preparing an income tax return. . . . The writers we have studied, however, give us a very different picture. A writer caught in the act looks much like a very busy switchboard operator trying to juggle a number of demands on her attention and constraints on what she can do. . . .

In other words, both cognitively and physically you are doing a great variety of things when you write, even if you are not consciously aware of them. These include composing new sentences, reading over what you have already written, considering and reconsidering what you will say next, vocalizing and listening, changing words and sentences, making notes and other plans, and reading source material. There are also many pauses, distractions, and interruptions that affect the speed and fluency of your work. If this work is progressing smoothly, you have no need to pay precise attention to what you are doing, and in fact it is probably best to become absorbed. If you run into serious trouble, however, you do need to consider exactly what you are doing and make conscious choices to do something else.

THE PHASES OF THE WRITING PROCESS

Most attempts to describe the writing process divide its components into three categories. From a cognitive perspective, Flower and Hayes called them *planning, translating,* and *reviewing.* Using a developmental model, the British educator James Britton called them *conception, incubation,* and *production.* In his article "Teach Writing as a Process Not Product," in 1972, Donald Murray referred to them as *prewriting, writing,* and *rewriting,* and in another article as *prevision, vision,* and *revision.* Murray's terms, like most others, take into account that in the whole course of completing their work, writers spend some of their time planning and envisioning what they will say, some time producing new sentences and paragraphs, and some time reconsidering and changing what they have already written. These categories of activity are often called "stages" because specific plans and conceptions for saying something come before we say it, and because we can only revise something we have already written.

To identify obstacles to movement through this process with greater precision, I distinguish five types of activity, which I call "phases" rather than stages, because they do not necessarily follow a linear sequence. The two phases I add—*editing* and *release*—make distinctions especially important for understanding writing blocks. Here are my terms with explanations of what they mean.

• *Prewriting* includes everything the writer does in preparation for composing a text or a portion of a text. Reading, conducting research, making preliminary notes and outlines, talking about the subject to yourself or to others, and thinking about the task are all forms of prewriting. Taking a walk or making a cup of tea can be a form of prewriting if you use these activities to collect your thoughts—to imagine how and what you are going to write. Prewriting might begin with a dawning intention, a sense of motivation, a desire to say something, or an assignment.

• *Composing* is the process of generating new sentences and passages that might or might not appear in the finished product—committing words to paper, but not necessarily committing them to the audience.

• *Revising* means both "rewriting" and "rethinking" what you have already composed. Revision involves significant changes to a specific sentence, to selected passages, or to an entire draft.

• *Editing* is almost synonymous with "proofreading" or "polishing." In the publishing industry, "editing" refers to all of the changes an editor recommends, including extensive revisions. Here I want to restrict the meaning of "editing" to very local concerns about word choice, phrasing, punctuation, spelling, and typographical errors.

• *Release* is the act of letting the piece of writing go to the intended audience, where it will become a piece of communication. I realize that this moment is not always clear. Writers often show their work to readers before it is complete, to facilitate revision. Sometimes their work is returned for revision when they thought it was finished. But in most cases there is an identifiable moment when we believe, at least, that the work is done and turn it loose, to convey whatever it can to its audience. This is the moment John Steinbeck recorded on Wednesday, October 26, 1938, at the end of the journal he kept while he was writing *The Grapes of Wrath* : "Finished this day—and I hope to God it's good."

I include this last phase due to its powerful and sometimes riveting and distracting effects on the others. A vivid example of this point of release is when you drop a letter into a mail slot. At that moment, what you have written becomes, like speech, an "irreversible" utterance, and all of us have paused at that moment to make sure that we want to release a letter from our fingertips. *Is this really what I should have said or meant to say?*

In retrospect, this moment illuminates the power and freedom of the writing process, because until you let the letter drop you *can* take it back (and many of us have). You can then read it over, decide to send it after all, revise it, or destroy it, and neither the intended reader nor anyone else must know what you have done. This freedom applies to all writing, in all phases of the process. Regardless of the methods we use, awareness of this freedom is what allows us to write productively, with comfort and even with pleasure.

three

Lines, Loops, and Delays

When you write, you lay out a line of words. The line of words is a miner's pick, a woodcarver's gouge, a surgeon's probe. You wield it, and it digs a path you follow. Soon you will find yourself deep in new territory. Is it a dead end, or have you located the real subject? You will know tomorrow, or this time next year.

ANNIE DILLARD

MAKING LINES OUT OF LOOPS

Some of the most disabling misconceptions about writing result from the linearity of its product: the finished text. In the end, a piece of writing begins with the first word and proceeds as a sequence of words, sentences, and paragraphs to the end, the last word. While we are writing, we are trying to produce that sequence, and for this reason it is almost irresistibly tempting to confuse the linearity of the product with the process, *which is not linear.* It is tempting, for example, to assume that the most efficient way to get from the beginning of the process to the end is to start with the first word and write continuously to the last, without interruptions or revisions. Reading strengthens this notion, this hope, because the product conceals the process. Lacking evidence to the contrary, we tend to assume that the first sentence we read in a book or article is the first word the author wrote, and that the "writing" (both product and process) continued in a harmonious, linear fashion to the end. In fact, that first sentence might have been added or revised toward the end of the process, or at any point along the way.

It is also tempting to think of the phases of the process described in the previous chapter as a linear sequence of "stages" of writing. This temptation is what leads teachers to prescribe the methods taught in many schools.

27

First prepare to write, by choosing a topic, completing readings, and making outlines (prewriting). *Then write the paper according to plans* (composing). *Then read over what you have written and make necessary changes* (revising and editing). *Then turn it in* (release). Completing each stage before turning to the next seems perfectly logical, and many writers continue to use such methods (or attempt to use them, or feel that they should be using them) long after they finish high school and college.

If the shortest distance between the beginning of the process and the end is a straight line, a sequence of stages, it also stands to reason that we can shorten the process by leaving out stages. Student writers routinely employ this logic when they try to complete papers (even long research papers) in a single draft that they might or might not proofread, thus eliminating revision and sometimes editing. *Figure out what you are going to say. Write the paper. Fix it up* (or *Run it through spellcheck*). *Turn it in.* This is the process my students typically describe. And in some situations writers can virtually eliminate prewriting as well. When we write informal letters, for example, we can sometimes just start with the first word and continue to the last, without preparations or changes. In these cases, the writing process seems to consist only of *composing*, in a linear sequence that directly becomes the product.

Or so it *seems*, if we don't pay close attention to what we are actually doing. If we do pay attention, we can observe some basic flaws in this linear thinking that can get writers into deep trouble.

In practice, extensive, continuous composing occurs only when we are "freewriting": the method Peter Elbow used to overcome blocks in his graduate studies and first described in his book *Writing Without Teachers*, in 1973. Freewriting exercises demonstrate that we can always produce writing if we remove the rhetorical concerns that disconnect writing from thinking. These concerns, about the product, include particular intentions, standards for performance, and ideas about what readers will expect. To eliminate these constraints, simply take a piece of paper and begin to write whatever comes to mind, even if you are thinking "I don't know what to say." Write that, and anything else that occurs to you. "The only requirement," Elbow says, "is that you *never* stop," until you reach the end of the time or number of pages you have set aside for this activity. Elbow recommends that we do freewriting for about ten minutes a day, at least three times a week, because "it undoes the ingrained habit of editing at the same time you are trying to produce. It will make writing less blocked because words will come more easily. You will use up more paper, but chew up fewer pencils."

This exercise is a good way to generate material and get yourself moving when you are feeling mired in a project, but it also illuminates what is really going on when you are writing more slowly, struggling to put language and ideas together. To understand why writing seems almost effortless in freewriting and terribly difficult in other circumstances, imagine that the mental and physical aspects of writing are two wires. By removing all of the concerns about the product that create second thoughts and hesitations, freewriting puts these wires together, and the single rule *that you cannot stop* holds them together. Thinking and writing become a single, uninterrupted activity, both mental and physical. The sensation, which can be very pleasurable, is that thoughts spontaneously occur in words that move directly from the mind to the hand, in a continuous stream, and tumble from the pen onto paper. Once this movement begins, it seems to draw more writing into motion behind it, like water pouring from the end of a hose. We do not first try to have thoughts, then figure out how to express them, and then construct sentences in separate stages. If we pause for these "mental" operations, the physical movement of writing stops, and the wires disconnect. Thoughts no longer become written sentences, and no longer reach the page.

In a sense, freewriting is what we are *always* doing when we compose, and explains how *all* writing first comes about, even if we continually interrupt this flow. Writing comes into existence through the convergence of language and thought, through the motion of a pen on paper or of fingers on a keyboard. When that convergence and motion stop, writing stops as well until the motion resumes.

These observations explain why you are rarely just composing and why the composing phase is rarely a separate "stage" of the writing process, even if you are trying to produce a paper, a dissertation chapter, or a letter in a single draft. Freewriting generates one or two pages of text in ten minutes, depending on the speed of one's handwriting. If you are producing much less than this, the flow of your writing is not continuous. If the flow of words and sentences onto the page is not continuous, during those interruptions you are not composing. And if you are not composing, you must be doing something else. There is nothing wrong with doing something else, and I'm not suggesting that you should be able to compose several pages per hour of writing time. *But there is something wrong with the idea that you are engaged in a single, continuous activity if you are not.*

What are you actually doing? You probably pause to read over what you have already written, to restore a sense of continuity and gather momentum for the next sentences. In fact it is difficult *not* to do this in most kinds of writing, as you can discover with an exercise that Elbow and other writers have suggested. To make reading back impossible, turn off your computer screen or, if you are writing by hand, cover what you have written with a blank page, and try to continue. If you are trying to produce something cohesive, you will probably soon feel you are getting lost and will want to look back. Most of us spend a large proportion of our "composing" time reading over what we have already said, and this reading often leads us to revise and edit passages we have composed.

In addition, you probably pause frequently to consider what you will say next—to let sentences form in your mind before you commit them to paper. Your hands become still; your eyes move from the screen or page. You might silently vocalize the sentences to test how they sound, then rephrase them in your mind before you write them down. You might pause longer to think ahead to the next passages, and plot out the direction your work will take. You might even get up to do something else altogether, and return to the task minutes or hours later.

In other words, *while you are composing you are also prewriting, revising, and editing.* Unless you are freewriting, therefore, movement through the process does not occur in a linear sequence of separate stages or in a single, undifferentiated act of "writing." Progress occurs, instead, in overlapping spirals, or "loops." Within the composing phase itself, writers usually move continually through "microloops" of planning, reading, revising, and editing. Those who are struggling with a task of composition interrupt this phase continually, especially if they are trying to make the first draft the last and if their standards for the finished product are high.

Examples in later chapters will illustrate how blocked writers get caught in these loops to the extent that movement occurs in circles, and progress ends. Blocks do not usually suspend writing activities. The writer is still in the process, often busily at work. When he was completely blocked, Paul continued to compose sentences. When he paused to read these sentences, however, he found them unworthy, abandoned that draft, started a new one, paused to read it, rejected it, and so on, in a potentially endless cycle. While hard at work, he could move through these loops for hours, over several days, without getting anywhere. I knew another undergraduate who had invested more than a hundred hours of work on writing assignments during a semester without completing a single page of continuous text.

EUCLIDEAN MYTHS

There is another basic reason for which linear conceptions of the writing process are false. The Euclidean premise *that the shortest distance between two points is a straight line* presumes that we know the locations of both points. Otherwise we can't determine where that line should start or what direction it should take. Even if we know where to begin, without a clear destination our straight path might lead us nowhere, or to an impasse. Euclid also presumed empty space, where straight lines are always possible. Real physical and intellectual terrains pose all sorts of obstacles, unknowns, and alternatives.

Detailed plans, outlines, and prescriptive formats appear to resolve this problem. The linear methods taught in schools attempt to eliminate the loopiness of writing by urging students to plan their work thoroughly before they begin to compose. *Figure out what you are going to say. Make an outline. Follow the outline.* The "five-paragraph theme" assigned in high schools defines a topic at the end of an introductory paragraph, divides the topic into three subtopics, elaborates the subtopics in three body paragraphs, and ends with a conclusion that typically restates the introduction. In other kinds of highly structured writing—such as scientific and business reports, some kinds of news articles, and formal correspondence—it is possible to plot out the direction of the writing to a known destination and conceive the whole project in advance. Scientific articles and lab reports introduce the research in a predictable form and proceed through explanations of methods and results toward conclusions. Such formulas resolve large questions of organization in advance and can lead writers to believe, at least, that composing is just a matter of filling in the blanks.

If plans, outlines, and formats eliminate the loops in the writing process, we might expect that people who routinely use these preconceived structures would not need to revise their work as extensively as novelists and other "creative" writers do. Indeed, authors of fiction and poetry often describe writing as a transformative journey into the unknown, as Baldwin did, or as "a process of discovery"—a phrase that dozens of authors have used. "A poem is an exploration," Robert Penn Warren said, "not a working out of a theme." Because these writers do not know in advance where their explorations will lead them, they are not following a straight, well-marked path to a known destination. "I start off but I don't know where I am going," the poet Galway Kinnell said. "I try this avenue and that avenue, that turns out to be a dead end, this is a dead end, and so on. The search takes a long time and I have to backtrack often." These and many similar statements from well-known authors are collected in Donald Murray's article "Internal Revision," which argues that writers find out what they have to say and where their work is going through writing itself.

Although plans and formats provide maps that give writers a general sense of direction, they do not actually make writing a linear process. Nor do they explain why some writers revise extensively while others do not. I suspect that on the average, professional scientists spend as much time revising and editing their work as novelists, poets, and scholars in the humanities do. Studies of scientists at work—such as *Writing Biology* by Greg Myers and *Laboratory Life* by Bruno Latour and Steve Woolgar—support my own observations that the experimental, exploratory nature of scientific research extends to the process of writing articles, grant proposals, and other professional communications that seem to be strictly formulated. In these forms of writing there are predictable blanks to be filled in, but filling them in typically requires several drafts and hundreds of editorial changes even before authors release a manuscript to a publisher. Then editors and reviewers usually require further changes, including what may be substantial revision.

The formats of business reports and legal briefs do not eliminate revision either. "I remember one all-night effort," a partner in a law firm told me in a letter,

> in which five of us . . . sat around fine-tuning a reply brief in the United States Supreme Court to reduce it to nine pages to avoid the strictures of a rule requiring that a brief of ten or more pages include tables of contents and authorities. The theory was that a Justice confronted with eight or nine briefs that were not at all brief would not be able to resist reading such a thin, short document first.

This night of "fine-tuning" followed extensive revision of drafts. Far from eliminating revision, the closed "strictures" of the reply brief made this work necessary.

Nor is it true that authors of more open, expressive genres always wander into the unknown, and "back-track often." John Irving is not the only writer who believes one should "know the story" in advance. The prolific novelist Georges Simenon completed each of his many books in about two weeks, in a linear sequence of stages: about two days for plotting the story, followed by successive days of composing chapters in order, one each day, and three days for revision. In a *Paris Review* interview, published in 1959, Simenon said that if he strayed from this plan for more than a day or two, even due to illness, he abandoned the novel altogether. When the interviewer asked him if revision involved "revising the plot pattern," Simenon replied, "Oh, I never touch anything of that kind. Sometimes I've changed the names while writing: a woman will be Helen in the first chapter and Charlotte in the second, you know; so in revising I straighten this out. And then, cut, cut, cut."

Within a format or without one, however, writers can't entirely avoid microloops, and the great majority of serious writers move through "macroloops" as well. In other words, prewriting does not end when composing begins, composing does not end when revision begins, and editing is not a separate stage following the completion of revisions. Instead, the process of composing a draft, or dissatisfaction with the direction it has taken, stimulates a new phase of prewriting, which leads to the revision of old material and the composition of new sentences and passages. Writers often edit sentences while they compose, and these changes can also stimulate new thoughts, which lead to larger revisions and even entirely new drafts. Like many other writers, when I've finished complex projects I can't count the number of drafts involved because I often stop composing after a few pages, develop a new strategy, and begin a new draft, weaving in passages from older ones. Word processors facilitate this patchwork, because we can easily move material from one document to another and delete unwanted portions. For those of us who work in this messy, "recursive" fashion, it is impossible to document (even to remember) the history of a particular completed text.

SPIRAL PROGRESS

For all of these reasons, we can't avoid loops in the writing process, and writers who try to avoid the macroloops of rethinking and revising drafts often become more laboriously engaged in the microloops of revising and editing sentences or paragraphs. The effort to make the first draft the last encourages us to pause frequently to read over our work and tinker with sentences, then to rehearse the next move before we actually commit a new sentence to paper.

Because these loops are unavoidable, so is the sensation of moving backward. In her 1980 summary of research on the behavior of writers at work, Sondra Perl noted

> that throughout the process of writing writers return to substrands of the overall process, or subroutines . . . ; writers use these to keep the process moving forward. In other words, recursiveness in writing implies that there is a forward-moving action that exists by virtue of a backward-moving action.

For progress to occur through these overlapping spirals, going back—whether to read over a paragraph, to edit a sentence, to read neglected sources, to revise a draft, or to plan a new one—should provide momentum toward the completion of the task. When you have picked up your train of thought, improved a sentence, gathered useful information, or found a new way to approach the topic, this loop should eventually propel you forward, beyond the point at which you turned back. And throughout that change in direction you should feel that going back is a positive way of getting ahead, much as the Voyager spacecraft used orbits around the planets to fling itself into farther reaches of the solar system.

Even for those of us who are used to extensive revision, however, going back to rewrite a draft can be frustrating and exhausting, not invigorating. And if you believe that the process should be linear, the feeling that you have reached a dead end, that you are lost, that you must turn back and start over, can seem like failure. When she recognized the necessity of revision, therefore, Alison felt blocked because she thought her paper should turn out right the first time, like a cake. Students in science labs often feel similarly "blocked" when linear experimental procedures yield irregular results. Rather than learning from these results and revising their strategies, as experienced scientists would do, they feel the experiment simply failed and is ruined.

The sensation of moving backward can feel like defeat, but for some writers it can also seem a relief from the more daunting task of moving on, composing new sentences, entering uncharted territory. Like walking, composing is a kind of falling into empty space. Just beyond the last word or sentence you write there is a void. You can fill that void only through release into movement, with faith that language and thought will converge in the moment, in coordinated ways that sustain progress. In this respect, freewriting is like walking without thinking about walking. More laborious, recursive methods of composing resemble the attempt to walk by first considering the challenge of taking a step and preparing to do so, by trying deliberately to coordinate your movements.

This effort to control abilities that are already coordinated has the opposite of the intended effect. Forward movement becomes halting and unsteady, and if you think too much about the complexity of the skills required, writing, like walking, can seem impossible. By analogy with another kind of movement, William Stafford explained the necessity of release, not control, in this passage from his book *Writing the Australian Crawl*:

> Just as any reasonable person who looks at water, and passes a hand through it, can see that it would not hold a person up; so it is the judgment of commonsense people that reliance on the weak material of students' experiences cannot possibly sustain a work of literature. But swimmers know that if they relax on the water it will prove to be miraculously buoyant; and writers know that a succession of little strokes on the material nearest them—without any prejudgments about the specific gravity of the topic or the reasonableness of their expectations—will result in creative progress. Writers are persons who

write; swimmers are (and from teaching a child I know how hard it is to persuade a reasonable person of this)—swimmers are persons who relax in the
water, let their heads go down, and reach out with ease and confidence.

For people who want to have complete control over the task and its outcome and feel that they do not have this control, actually composing chapters of a dissertation, for example, can seem dangerous. The knowledge
and skill required make writing seem an occasion for drowning. When you
sense that you are entering those deep waters, what should you do next?
Return to shore, the anxious writer decides. *Make further preparations.
Assemble the knowledge, skill, and control you need to make the next attempt more safely, with greater confidence.*

This stimulus/response pattern explains why writing blocks usually
(though not always) occur in the composing phase and carry writers back
into prewriting activities or diversions. Turning back often feels safer than
moving ahead, which might produce bad writing as evidence of our ignorance and confusion, or create messes we can't untangle. Better do some
further reading, make further notes and outlines, or simply take a break to
think about the task. Sometimes these activities can be useful, but writers
often return to them primarily because they feel comfortable.

For scholars, reading is an especially tempting escape from the struggles of composing and revising portions of a manuscript. Reading is, after
all, an essential part of scholarship, and as a way of gathering knowledge
it seems productive. At the end of the day you can say you accomplished
something, and can explain why reading that material seemed necessary
for further work on a writing project. There is no end to the amount of material a scholar should have read, or might find useful.

But why are you actually doing this or other things, rather than working directly on the text you are writing? In a moment of candor, a graduate student explained why he continually returned to the library to get more
books and articles he considered relevant to his thesis, and delayed writing for entire weeks while he read them. "Reading doesn't leave tracks,"
he said. You can tell advisors, friends, and yourself that you are working,
but no one will expect to see and evaluate the product of that work.

NOTWRITING

To describe these patterns of avoidance, postponement, and distraction,
blocked writers (and authors who write about them) often use the term
notwriting, or as one of my students called it, "nonwriting." In addition to

reading, making notes or outlines, and other activities normally involved in the writing process, notwriting can be almost anything we do instead of working productively on the task at hand. Watching television, cleaning the house or office, running errands, cooking elaborate meals, going for walks, calling friends, and other ordinary activities might be entirely unrelated to writing, but sometimes we do these things in a conscious or subconscious movement away from writing. Engagement in them represents disengagement from forward movement in the writing process. "When I'm working on a book," an English professor once told me, "is when I get my really deep cleaning done—like, behind the radiators." And sometimes these alternatives to writing seem essential to writing. In her book *Writing Past Dark*, Bonnie Friedman describes what she felt to be the necessity of killing all of the flies in her house before she could return to work on her novel:

> I wanted to get everything in that room just right before my writing began, I was afraid that just as a good idea was about to come to me, about to leap the synapse and appear full-blown, a fly would appear, and jar me, and the idea would fall in the gap and be lost forever, something impossible to recall because it was never really *known*.
>
> It was my very commitment to writing that kept me from it.

In retrospect, some of these diversions probably are helpful, and others are probably unavoidable. As I've pointed out, the writing process is necessarily loopy, and we can't expect to sit for hours continuously producing large chunks of writing without pausing to think, read, or relax. Distractions interfere with our concentration, but even without them we can't expect decent writing to pour out of us continuously like water from a faucet.

For this reason Donald Murray argued, in another essay called "The Essential Delay: When Writer's Block Isn't," that there are many good reasons for postponing active work on a writing project, even when long delays seem indistinguishable from a writing block. To examine his own writing practices, Murray kept a log of the time he spent writing over a period of forty-three weeks—301 days. This period was fairly productive in the end, but according to his records Murray spent only 206 hours directly at work drafting, revising, or editing. This working time was unevenly distributed. During ten of the forty-three weeks he wrote nothing, and throughout the period "I had more than adequate time," Murray said, "for panic and terror, doubt that I would ever write again, fears of writer's block, and plenty of time for the necessary incubation that precedes writing." These "essential delays," Murray argues, allow writers to gather information, develop ideas and plans, and reach the point at which they are actually ready to compose drafts. While long delays can produce frustration and anxiety, a headlong rush into a project can yield worse frustrations over disappointing, chaotic results and dead ends that sometimes induce real writing blocks.

I agree with Donald Murray that delays can be productive and that pauses in the writing process do not necessarily represent avoidance or procrastination. As I observed in the first chapter, people who stop writing for long periods of time, or forever, are not necessarily blocked writers. To entangle negatives even further, not writing is not necessarily *notwriting*.

When blocked writers refer to notwriting, however, they have become aware of a real pattern of interference with their movement through the writing process, even though these activities might seem, at the moment, essential to progress. Friedman felt very strongly at the time that those flies disrupted her writing and that killing them would restore her concentration. At another level, however, she knew that the flies were not the real problem and that the idea that she must kill them to gain control of her work was what interrupted her writing:

> Part of me craved my writing, part of me craved killing flies, part of me saw myself killing flies and said this makes no sense, and part said this *makes* sense, and part of me was aware of myself like looking at myself down a hall of mirrors. . . .
> I thought, If I can't control this room, how can I control my writing? Yet the essence of writing is not control, but release.

When scholars head off to the library to get another stack of books, they believe that further reading will restore the authority and direction they feel they have lost, and sometimes that is true. But those who return to reading and other forms of prewriting whenever they sense doubt or confusion are usually aware that the path to the library is part of a circle on which they habitually travel. Even if they can't resist this stimulus, they know that reading interrupts the writing process. Finding themselves on a familiar path, they can sense the difference between "essential delays" that carry the project forward in overlapping spirals and the circular loops that get them nowhere.

In many cases, progress itself is the stimulus that derails writers onto sidetracks of reading and other diversions. The graduate student who turned habitually to reading because it "doesn't leave tracks" made this turn when he felt he was *making tracks*: when his writing began to move in an interesting, original direction. When the wires of language and thought connected productively, he felt he needed to stop and think about what he was saying, to make sure he had the authority to say it. When the vehicle of writing began to take him somewhere, his first impulse was to jump off.

The "essential delays" that Murray appreciates are luxuries that some writers can afford more than others. Established poets, novelists, and some scholars can perhaps delay writing until they feel properly inspired or informed. As we will observe more closely in following chapters, most of the undergraduates, graduate students, and professors who struggle with writing projects have deadlines to meet, and those deadlines often draw the line between success and failure. An essential delay for Donald Murray might represent a catastrophic delay for an academic writer. Because many of the people who write about blocks are thinking of writing as an expressive art, outside academic contexts and constraints, their advice has limited relevance to those who write within academic and other professional institutions, such as corporations or law firms.

Methods, Standards, and Premature Judgments

> When I'm falling, I'm doing alright; when I'm slip-
> ping, I say, hey, this is interesting! It's when I'm
> standing upright that bothers me; I'm not doing so
> good; I'm stiff. . . . I'm really slipping, most of the
> time, into that glimpse. I'm like a slipping glimpser.
>
> WILLEM DE KOONING

MANY RIGHT WAYS

All writers move through the phases of the process I described, but they
move through these phases in a great variety of ways that depend both on
the nature of the project and on the preferences, conditioning, and habits
of the writer. It would be very convenient for everyone if I could use my
analysis of the writing process to devise a set of methods that would always eliminate blocks and other kinds of interference. Even in a particular type of writing, however, any two individuals are likely to use very different methods for getting from the beginning of the process to the end,
and these methods might be equally effective. In turn, strategies that lead
one writer into deep trouble might work beautifully for someone else. For
this reason, absolute prescriptions and prohibitions (*Always do this! Never
do that!*) often contribute to writing blocks, and those promoted as cures
for everyone soon ring false.

Several years ago, for example, I often told my students "Avoid editing
while you compose." This seemed like reasonable advice, and you will find
it in many books on writing. Editorial attention interrupts composing and
breaks the connection with speech that allows new, fluent sentences to un-
fold. As a consequence, excessive editing can entangle writers in corrections to the extent that they become immobilized.

39

When I paid close attention to my own methods, however, I realized that I frequently pause to edit sentences while I compose. Sometimes I hear problems in a sentence while I'm writing it and immediately make changes before I continue. When I stop to read back over a draft, to restore my train of thought, I also notice things I want to change and make those alterations before I go on. I suspect that most writers do this to some extent, and editing does not necessarily interfere with their progress. Clarifying and polishing previous sentences can also clarify our sense of direction and smooth out the path on which we move ahead, much as a ski trail becomes faster when the rough spots are worn down. I don't feel that I can continue very far if I leave rough, murky writing behind me.

Many blocked writers do become feverishly absorbed in editing while they compose, constantly rewording sentences until they become frustrated and stop writing. Dorothy Parker could say wonderful things spontaneously in conversation but wrote in an intensely laborious, editorial fashion, as her own worst critic. "It takes me six months to do a story," she said in an interview. "I think it out and then write it sentence by sentence—no first draft. I can't write five words but that I change seven."

Yet this intense editing that most of us would find paralyzing allows some writers to establish the kind of voice they want, if they have the patience to fuss with sentences without getting discouraged. In an interview published in the *Journal of Advanced Composition*, the anthropologist Clifford Geertz described methods that sound like classic symptoms of a writing block:

I hesitate to confess this in public because I think it's a very bad way to do things, but I'll do it anyway: I don't write drafts. I write from the beginning to the end, and when it's finished it's done. And I write very slowly. That may seem odd, because I've written a lot, but I've often been in situations like this one here in Princeton [at the Center for Advanced Studies] where I've had a lot of time to write. I never leave a sentence or a paragraph until I'm satisfied with it; and except for a few touch-ups at the end, I write essentially one draft. Once in a while people ask me for early drafts, but these drafts just don't exist. So I just go from line one to line X—even in a book. I have an outline, especially if it's a book, but I hardly pay attention to it. I just build it up in a sort of craft-like way of going through it carefully, and when it's done it's done. The process is very slow. I would not advise that other people write this way. I know people who can write a first draft and not care whether it's idiotic. They'll write "blah, blah, blah," and put zeros and hold space for something to be filled in later. Good writers do this. I wish I could too, but for reasons that are probably deeply psychological, it's impossible. I usually write about a paragraph a day, but at least it's essentially finished when it's done.

Geertz obviously compresses extensive prewriting and editing into tight loops within the composing phase, continually going back over sentences and rewording them until he establishes the polished, ornate style he prefers, then rehearsing and crafting the next sentence with the same microsurgical care. These lapidary methods partly account for the convoluted, "periodic" style of Geertz's many articles and books—a style that some readers love and others hate. Parenthetical asides and qualifications, built in during editing, break up the structure and often allow meaning and irony to flow back, from the end of the sentence to the beginning. Here is an example of the product, from his essay "Deep Play: Notes on the Balinese Cockfight":

> Of course, like drinking during Prohibition or, today, smoking marihuana, cockfights, being a part of "The Balinese Way of Life," nonetheless go on happening, and with extraordinary frequency. And, as with Prohibition or marihuana, from time to time the police (who, in 1958 at least, were almost all not Balinese but Javanese) feel called upon to make a raid, confiscate the cocks and spurs, fine a few people, and even now and then expose some of them in the tropical sun for a day as object lessons which never, somehow, get learned, even though occasionally, quite occasionally, the object dies.

Like many other successful, productive authors, Geertz suspects that his methods are wrong, that "good writers" do things differently, and that his own strategies are "probably deeply psychological." I argued at the beginning of this book that writing blocks are not reliably linked with, or caused by, any specific personality type or psychological condition. But individuals do lean toward particular ways of writing for reasons that are no doubt connected with their personalities. Some people need to make detailed plans before they compose even a brief document, and feel lost if they have no map to follow. Others feel confined by outlines and immediately plunge into composing in an exploratory way, with confidence that they will find a direction through writing. Still others, like Geertz, make an outline to find a point of departure and quickly abandon it, or outline their work between drafts, to make the structure of what they have written more visible.

For similar reasons, linked with personality and preference, writers sometimes tell me that they must complete a strong introduction before they can go on; otherwise they don't know where they are going. For equally logical reasons, others skip over the introduction and begin with the body of their work, because they can't introduce something that doesn't yet exist. And many writers compose a rough, "dummy" introduction to get themselves started and write a new one at the end of the process.

The comparative roughness of the first draft and the number of revisions represent other dramatic differences among methods, which seem to correlate with individual preferences rather than with disciplines or genres. The astronomer Carl Sagan, and Bernard Lewis, a well-known historian of Islam, both told me they produced the first "drafts" of books by speaking into voice recorders, as though they were delivering public lectures. They then transcribed these spoken drafts and revised them extensively. Sagan mentioned that *The Dragons of Eden*, which he had recently published at the time, went through about twelve drafts, with the help of extensive reviews from other scholars. A biochemist told me that he had about thirty drafts of his most recent article on his computer.

These drafts no doubt overlap in content, but if writers can count them, they must be separate documents, not the scraps of cannibalized text that remain when I finish a project. And messy as they are, my methods aren't unusual. In her study of "Revision Strategies of Student Writers and Experienced Adult Writers," Nancy Sommers included this quotation from a professional writer:

> I rewrite as I write. It is hard to tell what is a first draft because it is not determined by time. In one draft, I might cross out three pages, write two, cross out a fourth, rewrite it, and call it a draft. I am constantly writing and rewriting. I can only conceptualize so much in a first draft—only so much information can be held in my head at one time; my rewriting efforts are a reflection of how much information I can encompass at one time. There are levels and agendas which I have to attend to in each draft.

Some writers feel lost among these disorderly, loopy shifts between writing, rewriting, and prewriting and try to separate these types of activity as much as possible. Having made detailed chapter plans *for The Grapes of Wrath*, John Steinbeck completed this six-hundred-page novel essentially in one draft, composed in pencil, in five months. The journalist John McPhee, who writes long articles and books based on research and interviews, developed an elaborate rendition of the notecard systems that high school students are taught to use for writing research papers. In his introduction to *The John McPhee Reader* (1976), William L. Howarth describes these methods in great detail.

McPhee avoids composing drafts while he is doing research, because he wants to remain as receptive as possible in this phase. When he has completed his research, he types and expands his handwritten notes and assembles them in a large spring binder. Then he codes these notes by topic, writing each topic code on an index card, and sorts the cards into an order that defines the structure of the article he will write. With these cards arranged on a bulletin board, McPhee cuts copies of his typed notes into pieces, which he sorts into topically coded file folders. He composes his first draft by rearranging these strips and blocks of typed notes, moving from one folder to the next, typing a continuous version and marking his progress with a steel dart on the bulletin board. Because McPhee expends so much effort in developing and organizing his material at the beginning of the process, before he composes a full draft, he spends much less time revising his work and rarely alters the structure of the first version. Howarth observes, however, that this is not just an assembly-line method for producing articles. Instead, the structure he builds around the act of composing gives McPhee greater freedom in that act, where he can "move *against* a habitual thought or phrase, which is always the easiest, oldest rut to follow":

> . . . the main purpose of this routine is at once practical and aesthetic: it runs a line of order through the chaos of his notes and files, leaving him free to write on a given parcel of work at a given time. The other sections cannot come crowding in to clutter his desk and mind; he is spared that confusion by the structure of his work, by an ordained plan that cannot come tumbling down. . . .
> Structural order is not just a means of self-discipline for McPhee the writer; it is the main ingredient in his work that attracts his reader. Order establishes where the writer and reader are going and when they will arrive at a final destination.

Although most professional writers have settled into fairly routine work habits that allow them to produce the kinds of writing they want to produce, according to their own standards and circumstances, few of them believe that they have found the Right Way for everyone, even in their own fields. John McPhee did not prescribe his own strategies in the journalism course he taught, Howarth observes, "since he does not believe one writer's method should be a recipe for another's."

Preferred locations and times for writing also differ radically. Proust was so easily distracted that he built a soundproof room to create almost perfect isolation for his work. Steinbeck also hated distractions, but he liked the rhythmic sounds of Beethoven or the washing machine in the background while he worked, and I know many people who avoid isolation and prefer to write in public places, such as cafes. Some people always compose handwritten drafts; others use keyboards from the beginning of the process to the end, writing early in the morning, in the middle of the day, or late at night. Some writers feel that they can't concentrate unless their surroundings are perfectly tidy, but others can work productively in the midst of chaos.

What successful, experienced writers have to teach us, therefore, is *not* that there is a correct set of procedures we should all follow, regardless of our dispositions. On the contrary, their diverse methods demonstrate that the writing process offers us enormous freedom to experiment, develop strategies that work for us, and alter those strategies when they no longer work. In the wide range of methods that individual writers have found successful (and I've described only a few of them), we can see that there is nothing inherently right or wrong about outlining or plunging into the task, separating the phases of the process or shifting among them, producing multiple drafts or revising one, editing while you compose or reserving this activity for the end of the process. Whatever methods you currently use, if they do not work there are always alternatives, equally "right," that can work better.

The one characteristic that productive writers do hold in common is *persistence*, even when they are struggling with their work and with their own doubts about their ability. This quality of persistence, along with experimental changes in his methods, allowed Paul to move beyond a severe writing block, and it distinguishes capable people who become professional writers and scholars from those who do not.

Because the writing process is invisible to readers, we often confuse this persistence with "talent" or "inspiration." Perhaps there is such a thing as innate "talent" that contributes to the quality of a writer's work. What distinguishes successful writers from everyone else, however, is *not* that writing is or has become easy for them. They are accomplished writers, instead, because they keep writing, in spite of the difficulties they encounter. Writers who believe they will succeed or fail through "talent" receive this response from the poet Marvin Bell:

> The future belongs to the helpless. I am often presented that irresistible question asked by beginning poets: "Do you think I am any good?" I have learned to reply with a question: "If I say no, are you going to quit?" Because life offers any of us many excuses to quit. If you are going to quit now, you are almost certainly going to quit later. But I have concluded that writers are people . . . you cannot stop from writing. They are helpless to stop it.

Helpless to stop it? I agree that writers are people who have not stopped writing, but *helplessness* to stop still suggests innate drive, at least, if not talent. Whether they have that innate drive or do not, successful writers have found the time, methods, and resources in themselves to continue writing in spite of continual opportunities to stop: when a word, a sentence, or a draft goes wrong, or when they get criticism, rejection slips, bad advice, bad grades, or bad reviews. Those who are not helpless to stop have found ways, nonetheless, to stop stopping.

WHOSE STANDARDS ARE YOU TRYING TO MEET?

If freewriting exercises demonstrate that we can write continuously, almost effortlessly, what causes us to stop and revert to loops of prewriting, revision, and editing that make us feel that we are struggling with the task?

As I explained previously, freewriting works only if we remove the rhetorical constraints that cause us to worry about the quality and cohesion of the writing we are producing at the moment. These constraints include particular reasons for writing, conceptions of what this kind of writing should look like in the end, and expectations that our work should be clear or impressive to particular readers. If I tell students they must show their work to me or to other readers, therefore, these conditions impinge on the act of composing and "freewriting" no longer seems free. Writers become self-conscious and cannot stop themselves from stopping, to think about what they are writing and to assess its quality. *What will people think of this? Will they understand it? Does it sound stupid? Is this what I meant to say? Is it correct?*

In other words, we impose standards on our writing while we produce it, especially as we read sentences and passages we have already composed. Some of the questions we ask refer to the standards we imagine readers will eventually impose on the product of our efforts, and in some cases (such as formal assignments) we have information about the reader's expectations. Nonetheless, while we are writing, these imagined readers with their imagined expectations are not yet reading. The standards we impose on our work in progress are therefore essentially our own, even if we base these standards on reliable evidence. When you read over a draft you might say to yourself *This sounds terrible* or *This doesn't make sense.* To whom? Because you are the only person who is reading, these perceptions must be yours.

Sometimes these standards and critical perceptions can be productive. Continuous freewriting—without concerns about form, purpose, or audience—will not necessarily make sense, and a freewritten draft might need to be completely rewritten for a particular audience and purpose. For this reason, acting on your critical perceptions while you are writing can improve both the efficiency of the process and the quality of the product. When you read over what you have written, it *might* make sense for you to reconstruct a sentence, revise a passage, do additional research and planning, or start an entirely new version *as a way of moving forward.* I am not suggesting that you should abandon all standards for your writing while you are producing it.

The hazard these standards pose, however, is *that while you are writing you are not in a very good position to evaluate the quality of your work.* You probably know from experience that when you read something you wrote a week, a day, or even a few hours earlier, your perceptions have shifted. After this delay, you can usually see and hear more clearly how well the writing works and what kinds of changes you should make. Sentences that seemed perfectly clear and fluent when you wrote them might sound ambiguous or awkward. Passages that seemed ordinary, perhaps even confusing, might look brilliant in a later reading. Arguments you thought you believed when you made them might ring false in a later reading, or you might recognize ways of strengthening them. As a rule, these later perceptions are more reliable than immediate ones.

These standards become especially hazardous if they represent your expectations for the finished product or the internalized perceptions of some highly critical reader you imagine. Almost every sentence you compose can then appear to be substandard, and the resulting dissatisfaction and performance anxiety can make writing seem impossible.

This was the nature of Paul's writing block, and many others. I met a graduate student named Monica when she was in treatment for deep depression related to her failure to write a masters thesis, though no one could then determine whether her writing block was a cause or a symptom of her psychological problems. Nor was it immediately clear why Monica was blocked. She had completed writing projects successfully in her undergraduate work and in jobs she held after graduation. She had also coped with the challenges of living in three foreign countries, had completed extensive field research for her graduate thesis in one of them, and had developed effective plans for writing.

When I asked Monica to relate the history of her work on the project, she explained that several months earlier she had completed the analysis of her data and written a few pages of a rough draft. To find out whether she was on the right track, she gave this writing to one of her advisors, who tried to be helpful by making extensive corrections and revisions in red ink, as though this exploratory draft were a submitted manuscript.

The effect of this criticism was devastating. Because Monica used English as a second language and was not yet perfectly fluent, many of the advisor's marks involved minor errors and questions of word choice and phrasing. Others simply asked questions about her approach to the topic or suggested further reading, but Monica interpreted these comments as indications that she was not yet capable of writing about the subject at a level that would meet her advisor's standards. To raise herself to this level, she analyzed her data again, completed further reading, and made new, detailed outlines for writing. When she began to compose a new draft, however, it looked no better than the first, so she abandoned it, did further reading, and made new outlines. Continuing to write seemed pointless unless she could produce work that she could show to her advisor with greater confidence.

As weeks and months passed, therefore, Monica spent increasing amounts of time transcribing interviews, reading, making notes, and constructing elaborate outlines, until composing ceased altogether. All of this preparation felt necessary, but it brought her no closer to the completion of her thesis. Meanwhile, the end of her graduate support and student visa drew nearer, along with a mounting sense of helplessness and failure.

One of my colleagues, Barbara LeGendre, and I both met with Monica and exchanged e-mail messages with her over the following weeks, as she tried to resume work on a draft of her thesis. Our main challenges were to lower the standards Monica applied to her writing as she produced it, and to convince her that she did not need to make further transcriptions and outlines, her immediate recourse whenever she felt dissatisfied with her work. Because she hadn't produced any writing for so long, Monica also felt obliged to show everything she wrote to her advisors, the objects of her anxiety about its quality, and we had to convince her that this was not a good idea. Everything she wrote at this stage, we argued, was still private. She was not obliged to show anything to readers—even to us—until she chose to do so.

Monica thoroughly understood and accepted this advice, but acting on it was not so easy. Whenever she began to compose, the perception that her work was substandard reasserted itself and brought further progress to a halt. In an e-mail message she described the problem in this way:

> I hope you do not get fed up with me when I say "I still cannot write." But I have to be honest. It is true that I haven't written much yet. Issues remain the same. I simply cannot get rid of the idea that I want to write "a good paper." Once I start writing, I become very self-conscious. I start feeling overwhelmed by what I have to do. Yes, I know what you have told me. I do

understand the logic of the gap between "my standards and my performance." To connect understanding this issue and implementing it is another difficult task. It is much more difficult than I thought.

In another message she asked, "How can I JUSTIFY my writing? I mean, how can I judge that what I write is OK?" And later in the same message, "I would like to ask you again, how can I justify my writing when I don't feel good about it?"

I replied that while we are producing it, "Writing doesn't need to be justified." Through constant reiteration, our assurances gradually began to take hold. Around that time I wrote to her,

> From now on you might find that I just tell you the same things over and again in different ways, including things you sort of know already, until you believe them enough to put them into practice. You already know, at some level, that doing writing isn't something you have to live up to, that it has nothing to do with being right, that it isn't a treasure you have to find somewhere else, and that there's nothing special about it. All those ideas are what makes the little private fairly insignificant act of putting words together on paper seem like such a great risk, when actually it's probably about the least risky activity in the world, compared to most of the other things you've done.

Monica also realized that she could speak about her research with somewhat greater confidence, so she arranged to tape record a conversation about her project with a friend. This did not turn out to be an effective writing exercise in itself. During the discussion Monica's friend became critical of her approach, the discussion went off in many directions, and the recording was too fragmented to transcribe. Defending her research, however, did rekindle her initial enthusiasm for her subject, along with her desire to explain it to readers. After this discussion she managed to get a couple of pages written, and breaking our "rule," as she said, Monica arranged a meeting with her advisors to explain her difficulties and ideas. In previous meetings, she told us, she had just listened to their advice. In this meeting she talked and they listened, and to her surprise they were wonderfully supportive.

This and subsequent discussions with her advisors seemed to repair Monica's shattered confidence. They assured her that her work was genuinely interesting to them, and she realized that before she became blocked she had already written some finished papers and drafts directly relevant to her thesis. "I've realized that I've already written once what I really wanted to say. I have not realized this for a long time. Strange? But it is true that I did not give much credit to my writing products."

The objects of a sort of literary amnesia, these papers were never mentioned in our previous exchanges. Why? Because Monica had devalued all products of her effort, as she said, against an idealized, inaccessible standard she felt she should be meeting. "I have to have a treasure hunt," she once said. "But how can I find a map to look for this treasure?" Incessant outlining represented that search for a treasure map. When she had lowered her standards to the point that she could accept the writing she had already produced, Monica said, "Yeah, the treasure was already in my hand."

From that point on, Monica began to compose new material around revised versions of her earlier papers, and her work progressed very quickly. Less than five months after I met her, when she was on the verge of abandoning her graduate studies, Monica had completed her thesis, passed her exams, and accepted a job in her field. Signs of clinical depression had also vanished.

In the beginning I would not have predicted such a rapid, successful recovery, but I am no longer surprised by these breakthroughs. Blocked writers often write with great speed and momentum when they get past the obstacle. Like many other writers who have been struggling with a project for months or years, moving constantly from composing into prewriting activities, Monica was amply prepared to write. She never felt quite ready because she was trying to write according to the standards of someone she felt incapable of being. This effort to do the impossible depleted the energy, courage, and enthusiasm she had brought to challenges she faced in the past. When she accepted the writing she was actually capable of producing, with support from her advisors, all of this energy returned. Writing became, perhaps as never before, a fully embodied movement, connected with thought. "Writing is strange," Monica observed toward the end of this process. "It is a flow of my thoughts. I guess both of you have told me this many times. I now FEEL it with my heart. My thoughts are flowing. I myself am becoming a pen. I see a small light at the end of this long tunnel. I now just have to keep on going."

THE CHALLENGE OF GOVERNING EXPECTATIONS

During an interview included in *Writing the Australian Crawl*, William Stafford defined a writing block as an irrational "product of some kind of disproportion between your standards and your performance."

> I can imagine a person beginning to feel that he's not able to write up to that standard he imagines the world has set for him. But to me that's surrealis-

tic. The only standard I can rationally have is the one I am meeting right now. Of course I can write. *Anybody* can write. People might think that their product is not worthy of the person they assume they are. But it is.

Stafford went on to argue against the imposition of any critical standards while we are writing. "The *assessment* of the product," he explained, "is something that happens *after* you've done it. You should simply go ahead and *do* it. And do it, I might add, without being critical."

The skeptical interviewer, Sanford Pinsker, asked "Is there any point, though, in the history of a given poem—draft after draft—when the critical faculties of the poet ought to intrude?" Stafford replied,

> If I *had* to choose one answer and there was only one, I'd say "No! There's no point." That is because I would rather be wholehearted and be welcome about anything I write. The correct attitude to take about anything you write is "Welcome! Welcome!" Once you get yourself into the position of feeling that something that occurs to you is unworthy, well that's tough—because that happens to be what *has* occurred to you.

The things you write, he argued, should be expendable, "and the more expendable you keep feeling these things are, the more likely you are to have things happen to you." Stafford was referring to all kinds of things that surround and result from writing, and his analysis helps to explain why blocked writers feel generally immobilized, or numb. The effort to reach the point at which you can justifiably say something drains enormous amounts of time and energy from other dimensions of your life. When blocked writers lower their standards and become productive, this release into motion stimulates many other occurrences, including shifts in their relations with others, time and attention for other activities, and new opportunities.

For this reason I gave the quotations above to Monica (as one of her messages indicates), and I've recommended Stafford's *Writing the Australian Crawl* and another of his books, *You Must Revise Your Life*, to dozens of writers. I can't think of anyone else who understood and had alleviated writing difficulties so thoroughly, and his insights as a writer extended to teaching and to the whole of his life. Stafford reassures us that the life and work of a writer do not require the disturbance and struggle that Robert Holkeboer describes in his book *Creative Agony*, a litany of miseries that supports Kierkegaard's grim statement, "With the help of the thorn in my foot, I can spring higher than anyone with sound feet." Stafford demonstrates that through writing we can find a wholesome balance and composure. Here is another interview passage I often share with my students, from *You Must Revise Your Life*:

> It's possible to overlearn fear or overlearn confidence. The conditions of life are such that they make survival depend on the organism's ability to come back level again and be ready for the conditions of life as they are on the earth. . . . An individual's intellect and emotions should be like a good seismograph: sensitive enough to register what happens but strong enough not to be wrecked by the first little thing that happens. And so human beings have to occupy that position between being so steady and dumb and dull that they can't register and being so sensitive that they're wrecked by anything they register. So I just try to get into the readiness and be receptive, not stampeded, not overly trustful. I suppose we're all looking for that, but I feel the formulations that some people use disguise the necessity for avoiding both extremes. It's very easy to make powerful poems out of suffering all the time. It's all right; but that makes you a casualty.

And he practiced what he preached. Until his death in 1993, Stafford wrote almost every morning. He rose before dawn while the house was still silent, Kim Stafford recalls in her essay "My Father's Place." Then he made toast and coffee, reclined on a comfortable sofa, and wrote whatever came to him at the time—"no matter how trivial," he said,

> in order to get into motion, and the process of writing calls up other things, and a kind of train sets in, the sequence that comes about because I'm in motion. And every morning there is something to write about because it doesn't have to be much. It can be anything, there's always something.

When he had "run out of profitable moves" with particular poems, he sent the ones he liked to publishers, without worrying much about the outcome. Deciding what was good or bad, worthy or unworthy of being published, he said, was ultimately not his job. It was the job of editors and readers to decide what they liked and disliked. And because he produced a great volume of poems in this fashion, they had a lot to choose from.

Stafford's insights ring so true for me that I once imagined that if I simply shared them with blocked writers the problems would be solved. In theory they should be—at least for the kinds of blocks caused by critical standards and judgments, and by resulting performance anxiety. If you feel that you are not able to write up to that standard you imagine the world has set for you, in theory you should be able to lower that standard to the point at which writing becomes possible, perhaps even easy. In the process, after all, the only standards you have to meet are your own, not yet "the world's" or those of any other reader. In the moment you are free to raise and lower those standards, imagine or ignore the expectations of the audience, and make dozens of other adjustments that allow your work to progress. While you are writing there are no absolute standards you must meet, and if you feel blocked, the standards you have adopted are almost certainly too "high." I put this word in quotation marks because higher standards do not necessarily produce better writing.

My faith in this advice came into question, however, when I quoted Stafford once too often to a brilliant young writer who was constantly afflicted by her desire to write well. Something goes terribly wrong, I've noticed, when good writers try to be good writers, when smart people try to be smart, when a witty person like Dorothy Parker tries to be witty, or when we add an unnecessary layer of effort to other abilities we already possess. Good writers who are trying to be good writers usually sound as though they are trying too hard, because they are. The additional effort undermines fluency and makes writing itself a frustrating, laborious activity. Sonja was constantly struggling to find the right voice, the right subject, viewpoint, and frame of mind with which she could produce the deep, rich work she aspired to write, even though her best writing had been written almost effortlessly. Stafford notes that this struggle often results from a kind of vanity.

When I read Sonja a passage to this effect, however, I noticed a little flash of anger, and with a level stare she said, "Of course he's right. And of course I would love to be like William Stafford, so well adjusted and open. But I'm not, and that's the problem, isn't it?"

"No, it isn't the problem," I said, and then apologized for suggesting that in order to "find her voice" she needed to become a different person: more like an elderly, established poet who was no doubt born with a temperament different from hers. Trying too hard to make Stafford's point about standards I had missed it altogether. To move beyond writing blocks we do not have to get our lives entirely in order and become calm, confident individuals.

Academic writers have also reminded me that they do not have the luxury of saying whatever comes to mind at the moment, then sending it off at their leisure to see if anyone would like to publish it. They have to produce specific kinds of writing for specific purposes and audiences, often under deadlines. They are writing for teachers, advisors, and scholarly publications that send manuscripts out to authoritative reviewers. Producing a research paper, dissertation, or article carries risks greater than that of a rejection slip for a poem. The struggles these writers experience and the standards they impose upon their work result not only from their personalities but also from the circumstances in which they write.

In the next chapter I'll begin to describe ways in which academic contexts induce particular kinds of writing blocks. Before I turn to these conditions, however, I'll offer another literary example of a writer who managed to keep standards and judgments from undermining his work, even though he held extremely high standards and had grave doubts about his ability to meet them.

I mentioned previously that John Steinbeck completed *The Grapes of Wrath* in five months—one marathon session of daily writing from June through October of 1938—and in one pencilled draft. I didn't mention that this version was preceded by extensive research on migrant farmers, several newspaper articles on the subject, and an earlier, satirical version called *L'Affaire Lettuceberg*, which he recalled and destroyed after he had sent it to the publisher. Nor did I mention that throughout his work on *The Grapes of Wrath*, Steinbeck kept a writing journal, published in 1989 as a book titled *Working Days*.

Without this journal and other evidence, we might imagine a writer of extraordinary composure, always poised between overconfidence and fear like the "good seismograph" that Stafford described. At a glance, both the process and the product of Steinbeck's work support that impression. After all, in five months of steady writing he produced a long novel that won the Pulitzer Prize in 1940 and was the foundation for his Nobel Prize in 1962. Like Stafford, Steinbeck was an extremely productive writer during this portion of his career, and the great volume of material he composed each day suggests the opposite of a writing block.

By temperament, however, Steinbeck could hardly be less like William Stafford. A tense, anxious person, Steinbeck once confessed that he couldn't remember a day when he felt relaxed. Expecting to produce almost impossible amounts of fine writing each day, he became angry with himself when he fell behind schedule and continually judged his work unworthy. Throughout this period, which he once described as "a prison sentence," Steinbeck's journals reveal the same kinds of discouragement and fear that kept Monica from writing at all. *My work is no good, I think*, he wrote at the end of August, three months into the project. *I'm desperately upset about it. Have no discipline anymore. I must get back. An ordinary novel would be finished by now, but not this one. This one must be good. Very good. And I'm afraid it's not.*

> *September 7*: I'm afraid this book is going to pieces. If it does, I do too. I've wanted so badly for it to be good. If it isn't, I'm through in more ways than one.

September 26: This book has become a misery to me because of my inadequacy.

October 4: I've been looking back over this diary and, by God, the pressures were bad the whole damned time. There wasn't a bit that wasn't under pressure and now the pressure is removed and I'm still having trouble. It would be funny if the book was no good at all and if I had been kidding myself. Now forget the end and just go gradually to work. So long, diary.

October 19: *[When he was writing the last pages.]* I have very grave doubts sometimes. I don't want this to seem hurried. It must be just as slow and measured as the rest but I am sure of one thing—it isn't the great book I had hoped it would be. It's just a run-of-the-mill book. And the awful thing is that it is absolutely the best I can do. Now to work on it.

Working Days records a constant stream of good reasons to stop writing. How did a writer with such unreasonable expectations, low self-esteem, and harsh judgments of his ability avoid a writing block? We can find the answer to this question in Steinbeck's journals as well. "Now to work on it," he often said at the close of an anguished entry. "Now forget the end and just go gradually to work."

Steinbeck could not become a calm, accepting, confident individual. Even when he had concluded that *The Grapes of Wrath* was a mediocre novel, however, he continually set that judgment aside and returned his attention to the work at hand at the moment: the only place where writing can occur. He used his writing journal to admit and move beyond all of the disturbances that would interfere with work on the novel itself—to keep the novel from representing those disturbances. Like William Stafford, he understood that there was no point in worrying about the quality of a product he hadn't yet produced, or about the reactions of people who hadn't yet read it—could never read it if he didn't work on it now, wholeheartedly. "Forget your generalized audience," he advised in a letter to Robert Wallsten in 1962. "In the first place, the nameless, faceless audience will scare you to death and in the second place, unlike the theatre, it doesn't exist."

Although Steinbeck's methods and expectations created difficulties that few of us could endure, on good days, at least, he found momentary ease and calm in the writing itself, in spite of all the turmoil and doubt that surrounded it. In another letter to Wallsten, in 1960, he described this sense of *ease* in writing:

Today is a dawdly day. They seem to alternate. I do a whole of a day's work and then the next day, flushed with triumph, I dawdle. That's today. The crazy thing is that I get about the same number of words down either way. This morning I am clutching the pencil tight and this is not a good thing. It means I am not relaxed. And in this book I want to be just as relaxed as possible. Maybe that is another reason I am dawdling. I want that calmness to settle on me that feels so good—almost like a robe of cashmere it feels.

A writing journal can be a very useful place to set aside all of the discouragement and distress that might impinge upon your work, but otherwise I am certainly not encouraging you to emulate Steinbeck's methods. Relying on his wife, Carol Steinbeck, to preserve his isolation, he viewed everything as a distraction from his work. This "prison sentence" to which he condemned himself damaged his health and destroyed his marriage. The lesson, instead, is that if someone as compulsive and anxious as John Steinbeck could find composure in productive writing, all of us can.

Transitional Blocks in Undergraduate Studies

In response to one of the papers I wrote last semester, the professor added this comment: "This
seems to me a workmanlike treatment of the topic."
. . . It is rather hard to render anything other than
a "workmanlike treatment" of a topic after the format for a "successful" essay has been drilled into my
head throughout my high school career. A good paper consists of an introduction with a thesis, two
or three supporting body paragraphs, and a conclusion; doesn't it?

A COLLEGE FRESHMAN

DIAGNOSTICS

We are now prepared to understand why specific writing blocks occur and
how individual writers can move beyond them. I'll briefly summarize the
principles we can use for reaching this understanding.

Blocks are "psychophysical" obstacles to progress within the writing
process. In other words, something the writer is both thinking and doing
interrupts movement through the process and makes completion of the task
seem impossible. Blocked writers *act upon* misconceptions about the writing process, their own ability, the task at hand, or standards for performance. Successful writers such as John Steinbeck demonstrate that one can
have these misconceptions and still write productively, by setting them
aside in the moment. In turn, one can understand the nature of a block intellectually, as Monica did, without moving beyond it. "Cures" for writing
blocks thus require both conceptual and behavioral changes. While the writing process is ordinarily recursive, or "loopy," the stimulus/response pat-

terns that cause a block carry the writer back into repetitive cycles. As a consequence, blocked writers often work very hard, as though they were on a treadmill, without getting anywhere. This is why they typically describe the block in terms of immobility yet seem exhausted from the effort to write.

I've also emphasized that writing blocks occur in specific phases of the writing process and in a particular kind of writing task. They are rarely general conditions that affect all writing. Blocked writers have usually written quite successfully in the past, and they can usually complete writing tasks other than the ones that are giving them trouble. Even in this troublesome project they can often work productively up to the point in the process at which they become blocked. Although these obstacles usually occur in the composing phase, they can occur in other phases as well, including revision and the point of release.

If you encounter a writing block, therefore, you might feel generally helpless and immobilized, as though you simply "can't write," but the questions you need to ask yourself are quite specific:

- When and in what kind of writing did the block begin to occur?
- What other kinds of writing can you complete without so much difficulty, and why?
- Where, in the writing process, do you encounter a block?
- What kinds of activity surround the block? In other words, what are you doing up to the point at which you get stuck, and what do you do next?
- What ideas about writing, about yourself as a writer, or about audiences and standards, are associated with this problem?

Because writing blocks have specific causes, answers to these questions are highly individualized, but I can describe some observable patterns. The most general, perhaps, is that *blocks frequently occur in transitions from one level or type of writing to another.*

At this point of transition, audiences and standards change. Methods that previously worked often become dysfunctional. New types of writing require different strategies, and unfamiliar expectations create doubt about one's ability to perform. Long, complex projects draw writers into loops of revision that they have not previously experienced and make them feel lost in the process. All of these changes require both confidence and flexibility.

In following sections I'll describe some of these transitions and the ways in which they induce particular kinds of writing blocks.

DEVELOPMENTAL BLOCKS IN THE
TRANSITION TO COLLEGE

In the first chapter I mentioned that blocks have not been widely studied in composition research because writing instruction occurs primarily in the first year of college, and severe writing blocks are rare among college freshmen. This statement appears to conflict with what I just said about the transitional cause of blocks, since college freshmen are going through a major transition between high school and undergraduate studies. We might also expect to find high levels of performance anxiety among student writers whose work is constantly evaluated and graded.

These adjustments and pressures do create a great deal of confusion and stress among student writers, as Mike Rose found in his studies of undergraduates at UCLA. Rose concluded that writing blocks among undergraduates were essentially cognitive problems: misconceptions. The title of an article he wrote about his study—"Rigid Rules, Inflexible Plans, and the Stifling of Language"—suggests the kinds of misconceptions he observed among college students. The undergraduates who experienced writing blocks had failed to make necessary changes in their approaches to writing in new contexts. Debbie, a college freshman Rose quoted in his book *Writer's Block*, described one of the most common adjustments undergraduates must make to their conceptions of an essay:

> In high school I was given a formula that stated that you must write a thesis paragraph with only *three* points in it, and then develop each of those points. When I hit college I was given longer assignments. That stuck me for a bit, but then I realized that I could use as many ideas in my thesis paragraph as I needed and then develop paragraphs for each one.

Debbie recovered from being "stuck" only when she violated the rules she had been taught and devised a new strategy, more appropriate for the longer essays she was obliged to write. Eventually she would probably have to revise this new method as well, because it isn't always possible to include all of the paragraph topics in a "thesis paragraph." If Debbie had continued to approach more complex tasks with simple methods that had become ineffective, she would feel immobilized and incompetent: unable to do what she was actually capable of doing. The resulting frustration would then change the way she felt about writing, and about herself as a writer. The "blockers" in Rose's study had become wedded to ineffective strategies that seemed unalterably "right" to them, possibly because these approaches were keys to success in the past. Mike, one of these students, had developed ideas about writing that seemed more flexible and sophisticated than Debbie's, but led him into deeper trouble. Although he was willing to devise new approaches to an assignment in the prewriting phase of the process, he seemed incapable of revising these plans in later phases when they needed revision.

Mike's difficulties, too, are rooted in a distortion of the problem-solving process. When the time of the week for the assignment of writing topics draws near, Mike begins to prepare material, strategies, and plans that he believes will be appropriate. If the assignment matches his expectations, he has done a good job of analyzing the professor's intentions. If the assignment *doesn't* match his expectations, however, he cannot easily shift approaches. He feels trapped inside his original plans, cannot generate alternatives, and blocks.

Other blocked writers might act on the belief that they must know exactly what they want to say before they begin to compose, that they should be fully satisfied with every sentence before they go on to the next, or that the necessity of revision represents failure. Students in my undergraduate courses have often described anxieties and difficulties that sound like the symptoms of writing blocks. "When I write for others, I feel as if I were going to the dentist to get a tooth pulled," one sophomore wrote. "It is impressing others which cramps my thought processor." A junior political science major said he felt trapped by the knowledge and authority of his teachers:

> I have the most trouble using language when I am trying to write about something that a professor has said in one of my classes. I feel controlled by his words, somehow imprisoned by his thought, unable to reshape his ideas into my own. I have so much trouble taking the leap from my professor's framework to my own interpretation of the ideas that the process of writing is like vomiting all night long, over and over again. I have to hammer out every sentence at least three times before I will accept it, and by the time I finish a paragraph, I already hate the first sentence all over again.

This sounds very much like the experience of a blocked writer. "But then I will think of something," the student continued, "usually in the middle of the night, a new slant—my own direction—and the paper will be redeemed. This is the most difficult writing, but probably the writing from which I learn the most."

I believe that the overwhelming majority of undergraduates evade writing blocks, or quickly recover from them, primarily because they are young, inexperienced writers who must constantly adapt to changing expectations in their academic lives. In comparison with a dissertation, a book, or a professional article, the papers undergraduates write are also fairly short, and the stakes and standards are comparatively low. Undergraduates are used to producing essays under tight deadlines for authoritative readers, and while these conditions might be stressful, the product amounts only to some portion of a grade in one course.

Even the "blockers" Rose described, therefore, did not appear to suffer from severe writing blocks. "Dysfunctional rules are easily replaced with or counterbalanced by functional ones," he observed, "if there is no emotional reason to hold onto that which simply doesn't work." In three forty-five-minute meetings, Rose was unable to make significant progress with Sylvia, an undergraduate who felt that she could not compose a draft until she had crafted a perfect introductory paragraph. The stubbornness of her problem led Rose to conclude that Sylvia's block "was not exclusively cognitive": that it was held in place by emotional investments that might require other kinds of counseling.

While I agree with Rose that writing blocks are at least partly cognitive problems, linked with misconceptions, our understandings and misunderstandings are embedded in our lives, and there is no reason to believe that we can simply isolate and remove a false concept like a bad tooth. This is often possible for undergraduates because they have not yet become wedded to particular ideas and methods. In the midst of other changes, a new writing strategy does not seem very disruptive, and I have met with dozens of students who were, like the ones Rose describes, simply "stuck" temporarily. In an hour or two we could identify the cause of the problem, such as Alison's "learning disability," and find alternative approaches that these students were happy to try out.

Serious writing blocks are rarely simple matters of cognitive substitution, but they still can be viewed primarily as writing problems, even if they have emotional implications that require other kinds of attention. Paul's case demonstrates that severe blocks do occur among undergraduates, even in the freshman year. His problems with writing were obviously connected to emotionally charged memories of his father's criticism, and counseling might have helped to resolve those anxieties. Even without help from teachers or psychologists, however, Paul had figured out how to alter his behavior in ways that made writing possible.

While Paul labored under the conviction that everything he wrote exposed his incompetence, a college freshman named Carmen was severely blocked for different reasons. Having written successfully throughout high school, Carmen took a senior honors course that prepared students for the

Advanced Placement exam in English. The objective of this course was to teach students how to demonstrate that they knew how to write an impressive college-level essay, in response to an essay question. Carmen's teacher encouraged students to analyze the question by breaking it into parts, and to make sure they answered each part in a highly structured fashion. This emphasis on the formal structure of the product created performance anxiety and led Carmen to conflate the AP exam with college writing in general.

This idea that a writing assignment was a formal examination immediately derailed Carmen in college when she got an assignment on Shakespeare in her English Literature class. Having analyzed the question to death, with many pages of notes and quotations, she found that she couldn't represent that analysis in the form of an essay, and this problem confounded her in every assignment she received that year. In preparation for writing a simple three-page paper Carmen would produce enough notes of analysis and interpretation for a term paper in a graduate literature seminar, but these hours of labor did not yield a single paragraph of continuous writing. "In assignments in general," she told me, " the way I approach the *question* is the whole problem." Thinking about the question, its parts, and potential answers, kept her from *responding* to the question in writing. This, at least, seemed to be the most obvious cause of her problem.

Carmen could talk about her difficulties with the same kind of acute intelligence with which she analyzed essay questions, but several weeks of discussion did not resolve her writing block. Throughout these conversations she talked about writing as something she could no longer do at all, but she once mentioned in passing something she had written in her journal. She had been filling notebooks with daily entries for several years, she then explained, and still did so. She wrote extensively, in fact, about her inability to write, and the entries she let me read demonstrated that she could spontaneously discuss complex issues with great fluency and cohesion.

I tried to persuade Carmen that this was all writing amounted to, and that she should simply compose drafts of her papers in the same fashion, but this suggestion did not work. In writing she explained why, and in the passage below I've italicized words that reveal the standards for academic writing Carmen felt she should meet:

> My journal writing is informal and comfortable. It doesn't conform to anything. It flows freely in any and all directions. I write for myself and no one else. There are no expectations.

My paper writing is *formal* and *conforms* to a certain set of *standards*. Papers should have *direction* and *purpose*. They have an *image* to maintain. It takes a lot more work to *dress up* the writing and make it *polished*.

There is a vast store of things on hand to be put into a journal, but the contents of a paper must be created *on demand* according to certain *guidelines*.

When she gave me this comparison Carmen explained that writing a formal paper was like preparing for a formal social occasion that requires certain attire and behavior. And while she felt confident on those occasions, in writing they made her feel self-conscious and awkward. "What should I wear?" she said.

I met with Carmen regularly throughout her freshman year. Through many hours of conversation, our understanding of her difficulties with writing became increasingly refined. In these meetings and in the journal entries she let me read, Carmen observed that her efforts to write a good essay and thinking about the subject pulled her in opposite directions. And thinking, she realized, was by far the stronger of the two forces. Her high school experiences and the competitive atmosphere of college had led her to associate writing with "knowing" (demonstrating that you already know something), "whereas thinking," she said, "is an active process: it moves." Carmen explained this distinction and others in lively, eloquent passages that dispel any suspicion that she was incapable of writing well. In one of these passages she used the image of a "train of thought" to explain what went wrong when she tried to write formal essays:

I noticed that I can "feel" the difference between writing and non-writing. It's like switching tracks. It occurred to me that writing (putting thoughts on paper) is kind of like travelling on a train that is powered by thought. All I need to do is choose a topic (get on the train) sit down and start writing (thinking) (shedding new light on an old subject). Thinking always moves the train forward and forward only. And of course, if you're on a train track, it's impossible to run into a ditch. (Although you may encounter a few cows.)

Sounds great. Somehow I always managed to miss the train. I went back to the idea of switching tracks. It seemed to me that in the past I have stood *behind* the train and tried to pull it with knowledge. Number one, knowledge doesn't go anywhere, and number two, the train won't move backwards, even if I were strong enough to pull it and crazy enough to try. Well, it was easy enough to turn around. However, I still had (have) trouble getting on the train. Here's that in-between place that we identified. I quit what I had been doing and had a rough idea of what I should do instead, but it still didn't work. I could make the train move a little bit by thinking something, but then I had to catch up to it because I was standing on the tracks behind. Not a good way to travel.

In her French class, where her standards for performance were lower since French was a foreign language, Carmen could complete short essays, and in other assignments she could sometimes drag brief passages of "thinking" from her notes into the beginnings of a draft. She managed to complete one literature paper in this fashion, because the assignment was loosely structured and explicitly asked for her thoughts on the reading. In general, however, we made very little progress, and by the end of her freshman year Carmen's frustrations with writing were entangled with other aspects of a general malaise that a writing teacher could not address. She became increasingly unhappy with the routines and pressures of her academic work, and a year of study abroad did not change her feelings about the university when she returned. It seemed an almost toxic environment for her, and in her junior year Carmen dropped out of school. The emotional dimensions of her problems with writing seemed, as Rose would argue, to defeat "cognitive" solutions. As a teacher, I felt defeated as well. This was the first time I had failed to help a student who had continued to work with me, and in the end I felt that I had learned much more from Carmen than she had learned from me.

About four years later, however, Carmen told me in a letter that she had returned to school, at a small liberal arts college that encouraged creative expression, intellectual exploration, and communication more than competitive grading. In this environment, where teachers wanted most of all to know what students were thinking, not how much knowledge they could demonstrate, Carmen found that she could write. Lingering trepidation, she said, resulted more from her memories of failure in the university than from any real problems in this new, supportive environment.

In retrospect, therefore, I found evidence for a revised understanding of Carmen's writing block among my notes and recollections. The continual mystery we faced was the reason for which she could not *act upon* her conceptual grasp of the problem when she began to compose a draft in response to an assignment. This failure was especially frustrating because she watched other students "crank out" simple papers with shallow ideas that got decent grades in the courses she was taking.

Carmen knew that she was capable of producing the same kinds of papers with little effort, and she knew that this kind of assembly-line production was more or less what teachers expected of freshmen. Yet there was a side of her that staunchly resisted this way of writing.

In my attempt to understand this resistance I recalled that Carmen entered college with lofty, somewhat romantic ideas about what "higher education" should be: a free, creative exploration of the beauty and depth of art, literature, and science. She was the kind of student most of my colleagues say they want to teach—the kind of student who embodies the values of learning described in university brochures. One of her journal entries beautifully captures the standards she hoped to reach in writing, the nature of her difficulty in doing so, and her resistance to the values built into most academic assignments:

> Again, I need to let a thesis emerge from what I think. The process doesn't work backwards. What do I need to change in order for the thinking to work? Abandon the concept of theme. Drop all preconceived notions of elements in the text which would make good paper topics and/or examples. Don't focus on the elements, because that endows them with false significance. Those interesting and beautiful aspects of the work are insulted when they are treated like construction materials! Examining a text is not shopping for a paper! The author's creative genius tends to die when it's captured and exploited by someone with a writing assignment. Literature poaching should be outlawed. Of course, I never viewed paper-writing that way. I appreciate fine art. However, the tactics that I had been taught are geared towards completing assignments, and they messed me up somehow. I think that I just couldn't connect art appreciation and paper writing. I had it mapped as,

ART

WRITING   APPRECIATION

not as

ART   APPRECIATION   WRITING

From this perspective, Carmen could not reconcile her own values with the practical demands of meeting routine course requirements under pressure. Neither Carmen nor I could change the learning environment of a competitive university, and dropping out of it, into a more supportive environment, was perhaps the only real solution to her writing block.

FACING THE NECESSITY OF REVISION

In some respects Carmen was a precocious writer, because the kinds of difficulties she experienced arise much more frequently in advanced undergraduate work and graduate studies. From William Stafford's viewpoint, undergraduates rarely encounter writing blocks because their standards, and those of their teachers, are low enough to make writing possible. The great majority of college students strive to complete writing assignments in a single draft, often in a single evening of continuous writing. Although they usually revise and edit passages while they compose, they try to avoid the broader loops of rethinking and revising in which blocked writers become enmeshed. They feel that they must avoid these loops because they usually write under time constraints in the midst of many other demands, and they are able to do so because they settle for the thoughts that occur to them when they are planning or composing first drafts. A junior describes this aversion to substantial revision in her work on a thirteen-page research paper:

Right from the beginning I knew that my first draft was going to be my last. The only revisions that I made to the first draft of my paper were typos, and *occasionally* I would fix awkward sentences. There were absolutely no changes in the ideas, theme, and organization of the paper because they were already determined before I started writing. Part of the reason I did this was time constraints, but most of the time I just didn't feel like it: the sense of completion was so great that I just couldn't bring myself to go back and correct the paper.

In this entry from his writing journal, another college junior captures the moment when he chose not to revise:

Eight o'clock. I have the sudden urge to go for a walk. Clear my head of all that I have to do by next week. I'll be right back. And as soon as I'm back from wherever it is I'm going, I intend to finish this. Maybe I'll come up with an entirely new presentation. But that would mean I'd have to start the whole thing over again. Forget that idea, I'm going for a stroll.

As an undergraduate I became very good at maintaining a tone of authority and an appearance of cohesion in a single draft, even on long papers composed on a typewriter. Recalling occasions when I typed out twenty-page research papers in one night, with only a few handwritten notes to guide me, I have no idea how I avoided making a terrible mess. Word processors, which allow writers to make ongoing revisions and corrections, have further encouraged undergraduates to cultivate these skills.

But complex assignments in advanced courses eventually force many students to revise both their methods and their papers. This transition must occur when the quality of their first draft does not meet their standards for the finished product or the expectations they attribute, at least, to their teachers. At this turning point they must either lower their standards for the work they turn in or develop new methods that will effectively meet these standards.

As a rule, the undergraduates who become blocked make neither of these changes, or fail to make the latter change effectively. In other words, they continue to feel that they should produce writing better than the drafts they compose, but they have not found ways of writing that bring such improvements about. The political science major who felt "trapped" by his professors' ideas had entered this transition in a way that could eventually induce a writing block. While he was no longer satisfied with papers that reiterated ideas in lectures and readings, he was still trying to produce more original, creative work in a single draft, shortly before the paper was due, by starting to compose over and over until he found a theme he could pursue to the end. Under this pressure he eventually found "a new slant" that satisfied him, he said. But what if he did not?

Blocks of this kind are most common among highly motivated majors in the humanities and social sciences—in fields such as literature, history, philosophy, sociology, and political science. Advanced courses in these fields typically require papers much longer and more complex than those assigned in the freshman year, and writing, especially in the humanities, is the primary or entire basis for evaluation. At this level, teachers are no longer satisfied with the standard formulas inexperienced students use to crank out summaries and arguments. In specialized courses, literary interpretations differ in form and style from historical arguments, which differ from sociological, legal, philosophical, or psychological arguments. Majors in these fields need to learn specific ways of referring to sources, using evidence, and taking positions, especially if they hope to pursue graduate studies. And all of these new demands challenge approaches to writing that probably worked at lower levels of the curriculum.

Although I'm familiar with the kinds of blocks that occur in these transitions, it is very difficult to estimate how often they occur because most of the undergraduates who run into these obstacles either do not seek help or can't find it. A large proportion of the students who take grades of "incomplete" in the humanities and social sciences are unable to finish papers by the end of the term, and writing blocks account for many of these failures. Due to time constraints and other pressures, however, the writers themselves cannot always distinguish a block from procrastination, from the difficulty of the assignment, or from their confusion about the material, and neither can their teachers. It is difficult to predict what would have happened if the student had started to work on the assignment much earlier, had taken a different approach to the topic, or had more time available to spend on the paper. Failure to make up an incomplete, furthermore, does not necessarily mean that the student is a blocked writer. Lack of interest in the task and new priorities often explain why students never return to writing projects they failed to complete in previous terms.

The small proportion of these undergraduates who come to me for help have usually told their teachers that they were blocked, or simply that they were struggling with assignments, and were then referred to me. As in other cases of blocking, they say that they feel immobilized or mired in the project, and can't find a way to get through it. Students who identify themselves as blocked writers have usually been in this situation before, and realize that the problem is not confined to one assignment. Others have run into a block for the first time and have no idea why they are having so much trouble.

Using the questions I listed at the beginning of this chapter, I can usually figure out in one meeting why they have run into trouble and can offer some alternative strategies. And in most cases this is enough guidance to resolve the problem. As Mike Rose observed, these undergraduates typically follow specific rules and plans for writing that no longer work, often because the standards they are trying to meet have risen, or because the pressures surrounding the task have intensified.

For example, a sophomore named Veronica told me she had recently failed to complete three writing assignments, even though she had written for a school newspaper and received an A in a writing course the previous year. Suddenly she couldn't get beyond the planning stages: outlines, notes, and dozens of beginning sentences that she abandoned. Veronica's block occurred, as most do, when she began to compose a draft. Dissatisfied with this beginning, she stopped composing, fell back into prewriting, started over, became dissatisfied again, and so on. As the time available to work on the paper diminished, the pressure to write well at the moment increased.

It was not difficult to understand why Veronica had become blocked. In her second year of college she encountered more challenging assignments, yet she had less time to work on them. She was taking too many courses, all of them difficult, and she had extremely high standards for her performance. When she entered my office I could immediately see that she was exhausted and rather frantic, almost breathless. Because the intensity of her schedule had taken a toll on her concentration, when she started to compose she knew she was capable of producing better work, yet she didn't have time to relax and think about what she was doing with greater composure. Nor did she have time to run into trouble, so her aborted drafts added to the pressure she felt on the next assignment.

Acknowledging that she was overworked seemed to be a great relief in itself. I then tried to convince Veronica that she either had to drop a course or reduce her expectations. If she insisted on taking an unreasonable number of courses, she had to be willing to write what she considered to be "bad" papers, by going on to complete the drafts she abandoned. And if one of those papers received a bad grade (which, for Veronica, meant a B), this did not mean she was a bad writer or a bad student. It simply meant she did not have enough time to write a better one.

Although I talked with Veronica on campus in following semesters, this was our only conference about her writing problem. She did drop a course that semester, allowed herself to produce rough drafts, completed all of her assignments, and in later terms allowed herself more time to relax. Veronica's writing block resulted from maladjustments to the university environment, and when she reorganized her schedule and expectations, the problem was resolved.

For reasons that should now be obvious, the desire to impress particular teachers can suddenly block highly motivated undergraduates who have written very successfully in the past. These students are typically good writers who feel that they need to be better. They can imagine producing work more sophisticated and complex than the drafts they compose, and these standards continue to rise beyond their level of performance.

These blocks do not always occur in the composing phase. They frequently occur during revision and can even interrupt the process at the moment of release. One senior history major came to me for help because he had received grades of incomplete in three courses in which he had failed to turn in research papers. When I asked Jeff to show me his work on these projects, he brought in long papers that were essentially finished. He simply couldn't bring himself to turn them in, because he could always think of further changes he might make, further arguments and information he could use to strengthen them. One paper had grown in this fashion to more than forty pages, yet he still felt that it was not quite done.

Because Jeff could understand that turning in this "unfinished" work was preferable to failure, I thought the problem would be easy to solve. Over the following weeks he repeatedly told me he would give these papers to his professors, but at the last minute he always found some minor changes he simply had to make and postponed the release. I finally had to escort him to the department offices and watch as he put his work in faculty mailboxes.

Blocks can occur in the revision phase when a first draft does not meet the writer's standards for the finished product. Reading over this draft, the student recognizes internal contradictions, excessive formality, or alternative arguments and explanations. To make constructive changes, however, she might need to do further reading, assemble new plans, and thoroughly rewrite the paper. Dissatisfaction with the first draft carries her back through loops of prewriting and composing, and when the first version falls apart she might not see a single way of constructing a new version. She might see several ways, or clusters of ideas that do not fit together. Students in this position often show me many pages of outlines, notes, and disconnected passages that they describe as "a big mess."

Entering these loops of revision becomes especially frustrating for students who have invested a lot of time in making the first draft the last. When they realize that this effort was unsuccessful, the paper seems ruined. The block accompanies a fear that second thoughts and revisions will only make the paper worse, and approaching deadlines contribute to this fear of pursuing new lines of inquiry.

Because these time constraints are quite real, I can't always solve the immediate problem. My primary goal is to convince these writers that extensive revision is a completely normal and often necessary dimension of writing well, not a failure to write well. I also encourage them to break the habit of trying to finish papers in one draft, and to begin with exploratory drafts written more quickly, with less investment in being finished. Then revision becomes a predictable, welcome opportunity to reach a new level of understanding and expression. And if students begin to compose with the intention to revise, they are more likely to leave adequate time for this work, rather than feeling that the whole project has fallen to pieces like Humpty Dumpty at the end of the process, and it can't be reassembled.

INSTITUTIONAL CAUSES AND UNFORTUNATE SOLUTIONS

When they are resolved fairly quickly, transitional blocks are usually positive stages in the writer's development, toward more effective methods and more sophisticated forms of expression. "A first draft," one professor said in reference to his own work, "allows you to confront your own confusion about the subject. Revisions allow you to recover from that confusion." When student writers try to make the first draft the last, avoiding the messy loops of revision, they must pretend that first thoughts are the best. When they turn in first drafts as finished products, they either reveal their confusion or, if they are skillful, mask it. And by "confusion" here I also mean the suggestion that complex issues are simple, or that branching arguments and explanations can be reduced to a single, unambiguous position. Undergraduates who feel lost in a forest of possibilities when they begin to revise are encountering the real complexity of scholarship and, in some respects, the real difficulties and frustrations of professional writing.

Many students make these developmental transitions on their own. Others do so with the help of supportive teachers or staff members in campus writing centers. Unfortunately, I have known many other students who resolved transitional blocks by concluding prematurely that they were simply incapable of writing well in their chosen field of study. They solved the problem, then, not by changing their approaches to writing but by changing majors and avoiding courses that require extensive, difficult writing assignments.

Ideally, colleges and universities should acknowledge that transitions of this sort require both instruction and time. Teachers in advanced courses should help students adapt both their conceptions of writing and their methods to higher levels of discourse in specific fields. Ideally, courses should also include opportunities for extensive revision, along with the exchange of work in progress and other practices very common among the professions. Many programs in "writing across the curriculum" do include these opportunities at advanced levels of undergraduate work.

The prevailing notion, however, is that undergraduates should need help with writing only in their freshman year, when they acquire the "basic skills" required to pursue advanced study. If individual students have difficulty meeting these demands, we tend to assume too conveniently that they do not belong in that field of study. And while all scholars recognize the value of revision in their own professions, in their courses and assignments professors rarely make room for the recursive, exploratory methods most likely to produce the kinds of writing they value. It is very difficult for young writers to move beyond linear conceptions and strategies when they constantly write under pressure.

Academic institutions therefore contribute to transitional blocks in undergraduate work, and they often resolve these problems by encouraging students who struggle with developmental writing problems to give up. While I would like to guide highly motivated undergraduates toward more leisurely, exploratory writing strategies that would carry them to the levels of intellectual and literary development they want to reach, for practical reasons this is sometimes impossible. They simply don't have enough time to experiment, or in the midst of other demands the paper they are working on isn't worth the additional effort. As a consequence, developmental transitions that writers should move through, ideally, in their undergraduate studies are postponed—sometimes indefinitely, sometimes until they enter graduate programs or professions. Adjustments thus delayed and displaced to more demanding contexts in which the standards and stakes for writing are higher can produce writing problems much more difficult to resolve than problems encountered at earlier stages of academic work.

What Is Your Thesis?

There is the story of a Zen Buddhist who took a
group of monks into the forest, whereupon the
group soon lost their way. Presently one of the
monks asked their leader where they were going.
The wise man answered, "To the deepest, darkest
part of the forest, so that we can all find our way
out together." Doctoral research for the graduate
student in the social sciences is often experienced
in just that manner, trekking into a forest of impenetrable density and false turns.

KJELL RUDESTAM AND RAE NEWTON,

SURVIVING YOUR DISSERTATION

ENDLESS INTRODUCTIONS

Writing blocks in graduate studies, like those among undergraduates, are
usually transitional. In other words, they result from movement into new
contexts in which writing assumes different functions and forms, for audiences with different expectations. Writing tasks become longer and more
complex. Stakes and standards rise. Methods that were once successful no
longer reliably work. As a consequence, writers need to move through the
writing process differently, often against engrained habits and therefore in
ways that might seem awkward, unstable, inefficient, and hazardous. In
these circumstances, writers need to experiment and take risks; yet new,
potentially hazardous activities tend to make us cautious.

These general characteristics of transition apply especially to graduate
studies because the transitions at this level of higher education are at once
dramatic and poorly defined. Even the term *graduate student* sounds like
an oxymoron, referring as it does to someone who has graduated but is still
some kind of student. In the first two or three years of a PhD program some

71

vestiges of student life remain. In these first years graduate students are still enrolled in courses and complete assignments that receive grades. Course schedules help to structure their time, and most writing assignments are still "papers," due at particular intervals during the semester. In this period, therefore, graduate students run into writing difficulties similar to the ones that advanced, highly motivated undergraduates encounter. Higher standards and deeper investments in the quality of the finished product require different methods of production, even if the length and genre of the writing remain more or less unchanged. Students who do not make these adjustments in the writing process often feel incapable of meeting the standards "the world has set for them."

When PhD students have completed their candidacy exams and begin to work on their dissertations, however, rhetorical factors change in ways that greatly complicate, and in some ways mystify, the writing process. In the dissertation phase, therefore, struggles with writing are normal and writing blocks become common hazards, almost epidemic in some fields. Failure to complete the dissertation is probably the most frequent cause of attrition at advanced levels of graduate school, yet universities appear to accept this loss of many promising young scholars as a natural process of culling weak candidates. Writing blocks do not account for all of these failures—some of which are not failures at all, but decisions. In most graduate programs, however, there are several advanced students who are struggling unsuccessfully with dissertation projects, without asking for or receiving help from anyone. Although these difficulties sometimes occur in the sciences, they are most common in the humanities and social sciences, for reasons I will explain in a later chapter. And while I will refer primarily to writers in PhD programs, similar factors complicate the completion of master's degrees. Although universities tend to view these struggles as mysterious "personal" problems with writing, or as signs of low motivation and weak commitment to scholarship, the difficulties of dissertation writing can be described, and in most cases, resolved.

To illustrate the rhetorical factors that most often create these problems, I can begin with a retrospective account of my own experience.

When I returned from a year of research in India, as a PhD candidate in cultural anthropology, I looked forward to the rare luxury of eighteen months of fellowship support for library research and writing. Ample time, it seemed, to organize my research material and explain, in writing, what I had learned. The situation was complicated somewhat by the departure of my graduate committee chair and main advisor. No one on my new committee was familiar with the nature and context of my work, on the cultural history of the city of Lucknow, but this seemed in some ways an advantage. I was free to follow my own lines of inquiry with confidence that I knew more about the subject than did the members of my audience. And no one else, as far as I knew, had written directly about the elaborate connections I had begun to explore.

Now I can see very easily what I should have done from the beginning. From the masses of research notes, readings, and perspectives I had gathered around the project, I should have chosen a single, interesting question and used the dissertation to answer it, as efficiently as possible. In the time remaining under my fellowship, I could then use other research material to write articles, pursue related questions, and assemble broader perspectives for a book. In short, I would not have spent six months trying to compose introductions to a dissertation that was impossible to complete.

Why did I spend six months of my life trying to do the impossible?

With hindsight I can account for this period of confusion and futile effort with a few basic factors:

• I had previously written nothing longer than a forty-page research paper.

• As a consequence, I had no idea what a dissertation should be, how narrowly it should be focused, or how one should go about writing such a thing.

• My habitual writing methods, developed in undergraduate work, were fairly linear. I was accustomed to plotting the direction of my papers while composing the introduction and continued to compose following sections to the end, without substantial revision.

• Although my advisors were congenial and accessible, no one actively supervised my project or asked me to explain, in detail, what I was trying to do.

• I did not seek this kind of help, from them or from anyone else. For several hours every day, for several months, I worked alone, composing and rejecting a long series of unsatisfactory introductions.

Was I suffering from a writing block?

I was, according to the definitions I have offered in previous chapters. I was highly motivated to write and was fully capable of producing a dissertation based on my research. The block I encountered occurred at a particular point in the writing process, when I was trying to compose an introduction, and this encounter repeatedly threw me back into prewriting in circular loops. This block resulted from specific misconceptions of the task and from habitually linear methods of writing that no longer worked. Changes in my conceptions of the task and in my methods immediately removed the block and I began to write productively.

At the time, however, I simply felt I was struggling to do something very difficult yet necessary. Through my reading and field research on Lucknow and northern India, I had begun to see patterns that ran through the precolonial, colonial, and postcolonial history of the city, and also through the evolution of its physical structure, the relations among its religious communities, its distinctive urban culture, the conflicts between Sunni and Shi'a Muslims, and the political responses to these conflicts. All of these patterns seemed to be represented in an intense, volatile Muslim religious event: the commemoration of the persecution and death of Husain, the grandson of the Prophet, in the first ten days of the month of Muharram.

I did not feel that I was struggling with a writing block because I believed that describing these patterns was essentially an intellectual problem. To the extent that it seemed literary at all, it was a problem of introduction with which no one could help me. Before I could move on with the project, or ask for any advice, I had to introduce the multifaceted historical, cultural, religious, and political dimensions of my subject to readers who knew little about them. Although I felt in the process that I was trying to introduce five dissertations rather than one, for reasons I still don't entirely understand I could not see that the subject was too broad and unfocused. I assumed instead that I had not yet thought enough or read enough to accomplish the task.

So I thought and read more, tried to draft a new introduction beginning with a different facet of the crystal, found that this effort failed, like the ones before, to represent the whole of my understanding, returned to reading and thinking, back to composing, and so on in recursive loops that had become circles. In this repetition I began to sense, like someone who is lost and recognizes a tree he has passed several times, that I was getting nowhere. I felt embarrassed by the piles of introductions I had drafted, some nearly identical to one another, but I maintained the hope that a clearly marked path would eventually open before me, as one always had when I was writing papers for my courses.

Other graduate students at this stage were working in the same kind of solitude, and when we spoke casually about our work we all maintained the pretense, at least, that we were making slow but steady progress. I was at least writing. Some of them were still reading and making extensive notes, still preparing to write.

I have since met several former graduate students who had wrestled for months or years, more or less alone, with impossibly complex dissertation topics, became increasingly discouraged, and eventually abandoned their graduate work. This could have been my fate, but after six months I met with one of my advisors, explained what I was trying to do, and admitted my difficulty. He suggested that my topic was too broad and recommended that I focus the dissertation on the significance of Muharram in Lucknow— a single chapter in my original plan.

When I took this advice to heart and accepted it, I immediately experienced the first great release into motion through the writing process. With a central focus and question, I knew where to begin and what background material would be relevant to the subject. In comparison with my previous conception of the task, writing about Muharram also seemed easy, and I found that I could draft and revise chapters fairly quickly. Liberated from the belief that I had to explain everything I knew, and that I probably still didn't know enough, my dissertation now represented a portion of my knowledge within a larger frame of reference.

Unfortunately, the assistant professor who gave me this advice, and knew the most about my topic, was denied tenure and I continued to write without an active, informed audience. *Did my work make sense? Was it really of interest to anyone? Did it merit a PhD?* These nagging questions often undermined my confidence that I was doing anything worthwhile.

The second great release into productive writing occurred when three other graduate students and I formed a reading and discussion group. All of us were at approximately the same stage of writing dissertations on religion and culture. For each of our meetings we read and discussed one chapter from one of our dissertations, including its relation to the whole and common problems we faced in our work.

Without this group, I believe that at least one of the members would not have completed the PhD. All of us gained a great deal of motivation and momentum simply from the experience of having our work read with genuine, thoughtful interest. Because this was what we all needed from one another, we fell naturally into the roles of thorough, supportive readers who asked constructive questions, and we were so attentive to this task that I can still remember the chapters we discussed. The effects of this support were enlivening, and because we had to present chapters at appointed times, the group put our work on schedule. All of us completed our dissertations during the same semester.

Toward the beginning of my dissertation defense exam, one of my committee members asked, as he routinely did on these occasions, "I've read your dissertation. Now what is your thesis?"

It was a good question, and fortunately I had an answer. Unfortunately, graduate advisors too rarely ask this question when it really needs to be asked and answered, with attentiveness and support: at the beginning of the writing process, not at the end.

WHAT WRITERS NEED

With this example from my own experience in mind, we can begin to understand the main causes of dissertation blocks by first considering the needs of writers more generally. What makes writing easier or more difficult? When I ask people what they need in order to write productively, with comfort and confidence, their responses answer some basic questions of rhetoric:

- Who is writing?
- What?
- Why?
- For whom?
- With what authority?

To write with a sense of ease and confidence, we need to know who we are as writers—to establish a comfortable, more or less "natural," voice and persona. We also need to know what we are writing, and to know this we also need to know why: to have a clear sense of the form and purpose of the text we are producing. Clarity of form and purpose depends in part on our sense of connection to a real audience of receptive, attentive readers who will respond to what we say. And writing is considerably easier if we are trying to communicate something we know to people who want to know it.

For these reasons, people often mention personal letters to close, responsive friends as the easiest forms of writing. In these cases we know clearly who we are in relation to the reader and can easily establish a voice and persona that seems natural, without feeling that we have to pretend to be someone we are not. We also know what we have to say to these readers and why, because we know so clearly who they are and how they are likely to respond. Because we know what we want to say to these readers we can write with authority and confidence, partly on the basis of belief that they will be interested and responsive, not judgmental or dismissive. Most of these rhetorical conditions apply equally to speech, which is most comfortable, for most people, in conversation with good friends.

When I extend these questions to academic writing, most of my students describe one of two patterns. Some feel most comfortable and confident when they are writing in a very familiar form with a clear structure, about subjects they know well, for teachers who make their expectations very clear. Others feel most secure when they have freedom to express themselves with honesty, about matters of importance to them, for teachers who are genuinely interested in what they have to say. Although these patterns are in some ways opposite, both offer clear, positive answers to the questions I listed above. In both, writers know who they are, what they are writing, and why. They can also write with a sense of authority and confidence for readers they can trust.

In the dissertation phase of graduate school, if not before, all of these rhetorical factors can become vexed in ways that make writing very difficult. When we consider what people need in order to write comfortably and productively, the prevalence of severe writing problems among graduate students is not at all mysterious, though these problems are commonly mystified. To demystify them, I'll return to my list of questions in order, with specific reference to writing dissertations.

1. Who is writing a dissertation? Or, in slightly different terms, what kind of writer is a PhD candidate?

I have already noted that the position of a graduate student is in some ways fundamentally ambiguous and transitional, especially beyond the candidacy exams. In the period between those exams and the completion of the PhD, graduate students are, in a sense, former students and future scholars, or future members of other professional communities. As teaching assistants, they often instruct and informally advise undergraduates, yet they are not members of the faculty. They are engaged in research more or less at the level of professional scholarship, yet they cannot fully join the ranks of professorial scholars until they complete the PhD. In their dissertation research, writing, and other dimensions of their academic lives, graduate students are supposed to behave as though they were the kinds of people they have not yet fully become.

As a consequence, we can best understand graduate work not as a state of being but as *a process of becoming* a professional historian, psychologist, literature scholar, linguist, or biologist. Less a status in itself than a passage between other positions, graduate school is a transitional period through which one moves. From the perspective of most faculty advisors, successful graduate students are those who move through this transition smoothly, without much delay or difficulty. And in most departments the primary vehicle for this movement is writing.

In short, a dissertation writer needs to assemble the voice and persona of an established scholar for the purpose of demonstrating that she is capable of becoming such a person. Because we write most comfortably as some version of the people we imagine ourselves to be, the relative ease or difficulty of this task depends on the writer's confidence that she has something significant to say to an audience of scholars in her field and can represent herself to be an authority on the subject.

2. *What is a dissertation?*

It seems odd, in some respects, that this kind of writing remains so poorly defined, and that graduate students so often feel that they must invent the genre. Almost all of the professors who advise graduate students have written dissertations. Thousands of completed dissertations are bound and stored in university libraries, catalogued in dissertation abstracts, and occasionally cited in publications. These volumes constitute a marginal but substantial body of scholarship, readily available to people in the process of writing one. If you begin to doubt that you can produce such a thing, the library contains ample evidence that completing one is possible. And if you want to know what a successful dissertation in your field looks like, you can probably find some written specifically for your advisors. Surprisingly few graduate students even think of doing this, possibly because finding out what others did seems like cheating on a take-home exam.

But the general question remains: *What* is *a dissertation, exactly?* The difficulty of answering this question represents the nature of the genre, to the extent that it is one. And the ambiguous nature of this kind of writing is linked with the ambiguous, transitional status of the writer.

In their length, form, and focus, for example, dissertations resemble the types of scholarly books most often published by university presses, yet they are not really books. Publishers rarely accept unrevised dissertations as book manuscripts because they are usually too narrowly focused within a subfield of a discipline, or are too dry, methodical, and demonstrative to appeal to larger audiences. Dissertations are actually written for small audiences of three or four advisors to establish the author's potential, and in this respect we can think of them as "practice books"—as springboards or points of departure for further research and publication. No one has become an expert at writing dissertations. People write only one, and it is usually the first book-length text they have written. As a body of literature the quality of dissertations is, at best, uneven.

For this reason and others, I sometimes suggest that graduate students should think of the dissertation not as a book—certainly not as a magnum opus—but as a very long take-home exam: the exit exam, perhaps, for their entire lives as students. If the idea of an examination seems too daunting, I suggest that a dissertation is just a very long research paper or report. But perhaps it is most important to acknowledge simply that a dissertation is a transitional text: a way of getting from one point in your career to another.

3. *Why are you writing this dissertation?*

Writers' motives are usually mixed, so there is no reason to expect that those of a graduate student are pure. Scholars write books and articles to contribute ideas and information to their fields, to convey their own fascination with the subject, to raise their status in their professions, to settle scores with opponents, to build credentials for tenure and promotion, and sometimes to make money. But these mixed motives do not correlate directly with those for writing a dissertation. Instead, the problems of defining the genre extend to the writer's motivations and sense of purpose.

If you are writing a dissertation, your most obvious, self-interested motive is to convince your advisors that you deserve a PhD. This is a very good reason for *wanting* to finish a dissertation, but it probably isn't enough to sustain months or years of labor on the project. Scholarly and personal interest in the topic should add incentives, along with the desire to convey your knowledge and ideas to other scholars. But the small, sometimes inattentive audience can undermine this motivation. Scholars who are working on books have reasonable expectations that their text will be published, read by a few hundred people at least, reviewed in professional journals, and cited in other publications. Your dissertation *research* might eventually reach such audiences through publication, as articles or revised book manuscripts. The text you are writing, however, is likely to drop into near oblivion shortly after you complete it. If you pin your motivation entirely to that text, therefore, you are continually vulnerable to disillusionment. "Why am I putting myself through this torment?" you might ask. "No one is going to read it."

The most realistic and productive motivations acknowledge the transitional nature of this work and look beyond it. Why are you writing? To establish a necessary foundation for your career as a scholar, or for doing anything else that requires a PhD In this sense a dissertation is a working draft for the next phase of your life, and for this reason it retains value beyond its immediate significance as a piece of scholarship, in the eyes of its intended audience. The completion of your dissertation is one necessary stop on your way to other destinations.

4. *For whom are you writing?*

For yourself in some ways, for some of the reasons I mentioned above. But your primary audience consists of your graduate advisors, and your relation to this audience can have profound effects on the ease or difficulty with which you write.

In theory, your graduate advisors should help you resolve the rhetorical and conceptual problems mentioned above and generally supervise your completion of the PhD. They should make sure, for example, that your dissertation has a manageably focused thesis of interest in the field, and they should help you untangle other obstacles to progress with your writing. Attentive advisors should read early drafts of chapters and offer constructive suggestions, if necessary, for reorganization and revision.

For a number of reasons, however, advisors are often reluctant to offer advice. Even if they have published many books and articles over the years, they might not trust themselves to tell advisees how to write a dissertation because they recall that they didn't know what they were doing when they wrote their own, or because they feel uncertain about the effectiveness of their writing methods. In addition, the roles of a graduate advisor are somewhat at odds, as are the roles of all teachers. Both coaches and judges, they must finally evaluate the work they are helping students to produce. This awkward combination of roles often explains why advisors seem to withhold explicit guidance through the process of research and writing. Because one purpose of the dissertation is to demonstrate what you are capable of doing on your own, detailed advice might compromise that test of your ability. In the end, advisors want to feel that they are evaluating your work, not just the quality of their own suggestions.

For similar reasons, graduate students are often reluctant to ask faculty members for help in the process of writing, because doing so might be taken as a sign of weakness. Although it is rarely made explicit, there is a subtle understanding on both sides that the dissertation is a test of one's independent ability to complete a work of scholarship. To varying degrees, signs of dependence on advisors call that ability into question, even in fields in which collaborative endeavors are common.

The best advisors resolve these role conflicts, individually and collectively, and I have rarely met blocked writers who received thoughtful, supportive guidance throughout the writing process. Too often, faculty members provide little or no help, and their students feel that dissertation writing is a solitary journey into the wilderness, from which some people return, dissertation in hand, and others do not. Advisors who are not paying attention to the project and not communicating with one another can add to the writer's difficulties by making offhand suggestions the student hears as demands, or by conveying expectations that conflict with those of other members of the graduate committee.

Because professors in graduate programs are invariably busy with their own research and writing, along with teaching and other responsibilities, they tend toward conveniently optimistic assumptions about graduate students they haven't seen for weeks or months. In other words, they will assume that your work is progressing smoothly, that no news is good news, and that you will contact them if you need help.

5. *With what authority are you writing?*

Graduate students tend to delay composing and revert to reading when they experience any doubt about what they are saying, because they also tend to underestimate their own knowledge and authority over the subject. This is why difficulties with my introduction led me to read more about Indian history, Islam, and other related background material rather than to reconsider the focus of my dissertation. I assumed too quickly that my writing problem resulted from my own lack of knowledge and understanding.

When you are in the process of becoming a scholar in a particular discipline, it is very difficult to determine when you have read enough to be an authority or to make specific claims. In every field there is always more to read, and if you lack confidence you will never feel that you have read quite enough. Every academic book contains references to dozens, perhaps hundreds, of other books and articles the author of the book has presumably read, and that an aspiring scholar in the field *should* read, perhaps, before he can make knowledge claims with real authority. If he does not read them, any claim to knowledge or originality might betray ignorance. In *Writing for Social Scientists*, a delightful book with a deceptively bland title, the sociologist Howard Becker recalls how these questions continually undermined his efforts to write about his own dissertation research on the "professional culture" of Chicago school teachers:

I might substitute "shared beliefs" for "culture" and feel happier with that. But then I would see that I was talking about class and remember what a tangle of implications surrounds every one of the many ways sociologists talk about class. Whose version would I mean? W. Lloyd Warner's? Karl Marx's? I might decide to go back over the literature on class again before using such an expression. So I would put another sheet in the typewriter. But now I might notice that I had said "As a result of something teachers something-or-other." That is a pretty direct causal statement. Do I really think that social causality works like that? Shouldn't I use some less committing expression? In short, every way to say it would start me down some path I hadn't fully explored and might not want to take if I really understood what it would commit me to. The simplest remarks would have implications I might not like, and I wouldn't even know I was implying them.

Because these doubts can interrupt your writing in every sentence, and because the potential for further reading in a discipline is endless, continuing to write requires a certain kind of courage. At that moment of doubt you need to choose to continue. To make this choice comfortably, you also need to remember that while you are writing you are free to say anything you like, in an exploratory fashion. No one can question what you say until you release your work to a reader, and until you do so, your authority to say it is not an issue.

These factors to a great extent explain why writing a dissertation can be especially difficult, and one or more of them has been largely responsible for all of the writing blocks among graduate students I have known. When these misconceptions, ambiguities, and questions are resolved, writing blocks are usually resolved as well. Writing a dissertation remains somewhat difficult, as any long and complex project must be. For people who have been struggling for months to do the impossible, however, doing something possible seems relatively easy, and when blocks are removed writers often become surprisingly productive.

LIMINALITY

Because so many of these rhetorical problems are transitional, the dissertation phase of graduate school resembles what anthropologists have called the "liminal" phase of rites of passage, first distinguished by Arnold Van Gennep in *Les rites de passage*, published in 1908 and translated in English in 1960. Rites of passage—such as marriage, initiation, and graduation ceremonies—serve to convey and transform individuals from one position to another within a social structure. They provide a clear, formal, orchestrated response to questions that might otherwise be difficult to answer, such as *How and when do children become adults?* To regulate this transition, rites of passage need to remove individuals from one kind of social identity and transpose them to another, with a new persona. Van Gennep therefore distinguished in initiation ceremonies, for example, "rites of separation" from childhood and "rites of incorporation" into the ranks of adult men and women. He also observed that movement from one position to another is often represented by "liminal" or transitional rites, in which a bride, for example, is ceremonially transported from her natal home to that of her husband.

In *The Ritual Process*, Victor Turner gave considerable attention to the condition of liminality itself and to the peculiar status of liminal beings, separated from one kind of identity and not yet incorporated into the next. "The attributes of liminality or of liminal *personae* ('threshold people')," Turner explained,

> are necessarily ambiguous, since this condition and these persons elude or slip through the network of classifications that normally locate states and positions in cultural space. Liminal entities are neither here nor there; they are betwixt and between the positions assigned and arrayed by law, custom, convention, and ceremonial.

Liminal beings typically feel cut off from the roles, responsibilities, and securities of ordinary life in the society at large, and therefore feel vulnerable.

The last phase of graduate school certainly felt to me like a liminal condition, and to varying degrees it has felt this way—somewhat ghostly and disconnected—to most of the graduate students I have known. Opportunities to become stuck in this condition are especially hazardous because the liminal period of "candidacy" is quite long—generally two or three years—and because the condition itself is not entirely negative. The period of eighteen months set aside for producing my dissertation was a time of extraordinary freedom, in sharp contrast with the numerous demands and tight schedules of student life. During the hours set aside for my "writing" each day or night I had no specific responsibilities, no external constraints on the use of my time, no pressing deadlines. No one told me what this "work" on my dissertation should entail, how it should progress, what or how much I should read, or when I should have something written. In that liminal period, scholarship was divorced from performance and competition.

And in some ways scholarship without performance is an ideal exis-

tence. People commonly enter graduate programs because they enjoy learning, reading, thinking, and talking with others who have common interests.
They do not necessarily enjoy putting their knowledge and ideas out in
public written forms, where they are subject to scrutiny and potential criticism. The public, promotional, competitive, and often political dimensions
of scholarship can be unpleasant, even dangerous. As a consequence, the
diversions that represent a writing block can feel much safer and more ap-
pealing than actually writing something others will read.

I began to understand this appeal through my work with Carl, a graduate student who always seemed to need more information, or to refresh his
memory of books and articles he had already read. In effect, writing was
primarily a stimulus for further reading. Carl routinely produced a page or
two of perfectly coherent writing and would then stop composing for several days while he read material he considered essential to further work on
a draft. When he eventually returned to writing, however, his perspective
had shifted; he had developed slightly different (usually more intricate) arguments and explanations. So he started a new draft, became dissatisfied
after a couple of pages, and concluded once again that further reading would
solve the problem. Because Carl produced so little writing and had already
turned away from it by the time he showed it to me, our conversations also
turned to the material he was reading and its potential bearing on work he
had not yet produced. Although I told him each week that he should just
continue to write, he always convinced himself that a particular book (or
two or three) held the key to progress and was worth the delay.

Having heard these explanations for several weeks, I revealed my own
frustration and said, "Look, Carl. Writing is this little fire you tend, and
your goal is to keep it going. Maybe you have to leave it briefly to get a
few sticks, or a rabbit to cook, but just do that and hurry back before it
goes out. You don't want to spend days collecting several cords of fire-
wood or studying the principles of firebuilding. If you do, each time you
come back you'll have nothing but cold ashes."

Carl listened to this speech with growing discomfort. And after a moment of silence he sheepishly admitted, "I think I'm the rabbit."

He then explained that when he was writing, he felt more like the hunted
than the hunter. By comparison, reading was very safe. The real predators
from this viewpoint—the experienced scholars in your field—can't locate
your position if you avoid indicating where it is.

But Carl helped me to recognize that this attraction to what we might
think of as "pure scholarship" is not just a form of avoidance. It is also a
genuine pleasure and comfort. As students, we are trained primarily to read,

to study, to absorb information and ideas from authoritative sources; we also learn to write primarily as readers, about the work of established scholars: what is already known and has already been said. Without any impending demands for performance, how can you know when you are ready to take definitive positions in writing, when there is so much more to read, when there are so many new perspectives to consider?

I have met graduate students who were simply unwilling to trade the immediate pleasure and security of learning for the longer-term benefits of writing, even when they faced potential failure to complete their degrees. As long as they were learning, they felt they were making progress toward the eventual moment when they were ready to produce works of real scholarly authority. They could not acknowledge that without writing, reading and thinking did not get them anywhere. "Pure scholarship," cut off from engagement with real audiences and contexts, represents the liminal condition through which graduate students must move as writers.

This is why blocked writers are often the most knowledgeable, thoughtful, and potentially successful young scholars in a department, even though they keep this potential largely to themselves. They are the kinds of people universities and disciplines should not want to lose through neglect, yet they routinely do, in spite of their great investments in bringing PhD students to this last phase of their graduate work.

If faculty advisors, departments, and graduate schools acknowledged this potential value and unnecessary loss, along with the liminal nature of the dissertation phase, they could greatly reduce writing blocks, costly delays, attrition, and distress among their students. In this phase of graduate work, departments need to establish "rites of transition," in effect, to facilitate movement through the writing process and provide some of the rhetorical conditions that make writing more productive and engaging.

These support structures sometimes exist. Some departments define the oral candidacy exam, around the third year of a PhD program, as a defense of the dissertation proposal. This formal occasion ensures that candidates will formulate an early proposal and that advisors will read it, with an opportunity for the entire committee to negotiate expectations and modifications before the student begins to write. Some departments also organize colloquia in which PhD candidates present work in progress to students and faculty for discussion. These events help to create a real sense of audience for the writing and often bring the project into sharper focus. Chairs of graduate committees occasionally schedule stages of writing and committee meetings to keep their students on track. Faculty members assigned to direct graduate studies in their departments sometimes pay close attention to the progress of dissertation writers and intervene when they have become mired in their projects. I also know of departments that strongly encourage advanced graduate students to form writing groups like the one my friends and I developed on our own.

Unfortunately, these cases of active supervision and support remain exceptional in many fields of study, partly because PhD candidates themselves often resist them and want most of all to be left alone with their work. To the extent that dissertation projects represent specialized endeavors between individual students and individual professors, departments often conclude that they should not or cannot regulate these relations. As a consequence, individuals who are having difficulty with their projects and/or with their advisors feel cut off from other forms of support and from one another.

RHETORICAL SUPPORTS IN THE SCIENCES

Considering the rhetorical causes of most writing blocks among graduate students, it isn't entirely surprising that these problems arise more frequently in the humanities and social sciences than in the sciences. The main reasons concern differences in writing practices and epistemologies among these fields.

Most branches of the humanities and some of the social sciences maintain the working assumption that knowledge is constructed, interpreted, and exchanged through the medium of the individually authored text. Conversations, conferences, and other kinds of social exchange inform these endeavors, but when scholars in these fields are working on a book they tend to vanish into the library or into their offices and studies, where they read, think, and write in solitude. Their colleagues and students know what these individual scholars have written once it is published, but they rarely know how that writing comes about or what the writer is currently producing. Both research and writing are for the most part individual, private activities. A scholar's stature results from the volume and quality of the work produced in this solitary, rather mysterious fashion.

These features of scholarship and writing gradually change as we move through the social sciences and into the sciences, where research and writing are typically collaborative, social endeavors. In the experimental sciences and in related fields such as cognitive psychology, faculty members, postdoctoral fellows, graduate students, and occasionally undergraduates work together on research projects that eventually yield jointly authored articles. Writing practices vary a great deal from one research group to an-

other, as do the size of the research team, the amount of writing they produce, and the number of authors listed on publications. Some "principle
investigators" ask individual members of the group to draft specific sections and then supervise revisions. Others draft the article themselves or
ask a particular colleague to do so, and then distribute the draft to other
members of the group for suggestions. In any case, work in progress usually goes through collaborative revision, often in response to criticism from
external peer reviews or advice from colleagues at other institutions. As
Greg Myers observes in *Writing Biology*, research articles often go through
dozens of revisions before they are submitted, frequently rejected, and substantially revised again for resubmission. Many readers, in and outside the
research group, contribute to these changes.

In the sciences, therefore, graduate students have often become members of research and publication teams long before they begin to write their
dissertations, and their dissertation research usually emerges from work
they have been doing with professors and other students for some time.
Many have previously coauthored a number of professional articles on earlier stages of this research and have presented their findings at professional
conferences. Through these collaborative activities, they have gradually become professionals in their fields and have learned, through practice and
observation, how professional writing comes about. Because they are in
frequent contact with advisors and peers during their research, they typically feel they can show drafts of their work to informed readers or discuss problems they encounter whenever they need advice. These exchanges
reduce the isolation of graduate studies and satisfy many of the rhetorical
needs I noted above.

In addition, the text itself does not carry the kind of epistemological
weight in the sciences that it bears in the humanities. Publications are still
very important, as credentials for jobs and promotions, and professional
writing in the sciences undergoes intense scrutiny prior to publication. But
scientists tend to view written accounts of their research as somewhat epiphe-
nomenal constructions of knowledge they have assembled elsewhere, prior
to the writing of an article or dissertation. As a consequence, writing does
not hold the potentially paralyzing significance it can represent for authors
in the humanities, who often feel that if they can't assemble profound insights in the production of a text they essentially have nothing to say.

These contrasts became striking on one occasion when a graduate student in physics told me he was on his way to file his completed dissertation with the graduate school. I shook his hand, congratulated him, and
said, "It must be a tremendous relief to have the thing written."

He looked slightly puzzled by my enthusiasm and said, "Not really. It's mostly just my published articles stapled together." This wasn't literally true, of course, but through exaggeration he emphasized that by the time he started writing most of the hard work was already done.

I do not mean that graduate work is easier in the sciences than in the humanities. Many kinds of conceptual, methodological, and social problems can arise in the process of doing research, and these problems can delay or even prevent the completion of a PhD. One might say that scientists who cannot identify focused research questions or those who find themselves at an impasse during their investigations are suffering from "science blocks." But these problems do not tend to arise in the writing process, and scientists rarely think of them as writing problems. From their perspective, their research works or fails to work, progresses or does not progress, in the lab, in theoretical formulations, or in data analysis. Dissertation research in the sciences can become a liminal condition, but this usually means that graduate students are mired in experimental procedures or field studies that seem to be getting them nowhere, or that they are stuck in dysfunctional research groups—not that they are mired in the "writing up" of research they have largely completed.

The exceptions I can recall illustrate the rule. In other words, when scientists become derailed in the writing process, they have usually experienced the same kinds of rhetorical problems that more frequently afflict people in fields such as English, history, philosophy, or political studies. While writing, for one reason or another they have become isolated from advisors and peers. In this isolation, the focus and the dimensions of the project have become ambiguous, sometimes because these writers are trying to meet unreasonable expectations, real or imagined, from their faculty advisors.

During one semester, for example, I met occasionally with two science graduate students who had reached dead ends with their dissertations for similar reasons. Both had completed interesting research projects that had interdisciplinary implications, and as a consequence both had advisors in more than one department. The members of their graduate committees, in turn, had little or no contact with one another, and the chairs of these committees were paying very little attention to their progress.

One of these students, a physicist, had advisors in three departments who did not really know one another and had very different interests in the applications of the experimental procedures she had developed—applications that ranged from astrophysics to a branch of chemical engineering. When she asked these advisors individually what they would like to see in her dissertation, they naturally emphasized material most relevant to their own fields of study. Because each of these three dimensions of her research required particular kinds of data analysis, literature review, and discussion, this student felt that she needed, in effect, to write three dissertations, yet tie them together in a cohesive text.

The other graduate student, in neuroscience, had research interests and advisors in two departments. In addition, one of his key advisors and research associates had recently taken a position at another university and had stopped responding to e-mail requests for help with the project, including responses to portions of his manuscript. Because the student felt that he could not develop cohesive research claims without support from this former associate, real progress with his dissertation had come to a halt, yet he felt that he must try to assemble the two halves of the project until he received the help he needed. Without signs of interest from a key advisor, however, he began to feel that his research was of little significance.

Because both of these students were trying to do the impossible, I gradually persuaded them that they could each expect to write only one dissertation, not two or three, and that their advisors were responsible for making this integration possible. I encouraged them to ask very directly for this kind of help, after asking themselves what they would like the central focus and structure of this dissertation to be.

Having decided that she wanted to emphasize her experimental procedures, with single chapters on their applications, the physicist proposed this plan to each of her advisors and received their approval. One of them apologized for leading her to believe that he wanted elaborate analysis and discussion in his field, and explained that he was referring to further research and publication, not necessarily to her dissertation. This is an extremely common source of misunderstanding. When her writing project was thus reduced to a reasonable scale and focus, involving analysis she had already completed, work progressed very quickly and she finished her dissertation in about three months. In the markets for teaching jobs and postdoctoral fellowships, the interdisciplinary breadth that led to her writing problems became a great asset, and she received offers for three positions.

The neuroscientist, in turn, decided that he could not waste further time waiting for help essential to his writing. Summoning his courage, with the resolve that he would find a new committee member if he could not get active support, he telephoned his uncommunicative advisor. To his relief, his advisor was deeply apologetic, offered a long list of reasons for his silence, and reaffirmed his enthusiasm for the project. Because this advisor quickly read the material and offered valuable suggestions for integrating its dimensions, the student was able to write productively, finished the dissertation in five months, and pursued the research with a postdoctoral fellowship.

The speed with which these scientists completed successful dissertations demonstrates that they were very capable writers, temporarily blocked by circumstances over which they had more control than they imagined. When they acknowledged and took steps to change these circumstantial causes of their writing problems, they immediately began to use abilities that had been undermined by their efforts to do something unnecessarily difficult, if not impossible. In the next chapter we will examine these causes and effects more closely.

I have known graduate students and professors who initially entered the sciences partly to avoid writing, which they associated with the humanities. If they view themselves as weak writers, this avoidance sometimes undermines their confidence and continues to make the process of writing very difficult, the products awkward and hesitant. This pattern of avoidance can, in rare cases, lead to blocks if the writer feels reluctant to say anything for fear of revealing just how bad his writing is.

If blocks resulted from aversions to writing, weak skills in "English," or low confidence in one's writing ability, we would expect writing blocks to be at least as common in the sciences as in other sectors of higher education. Instead, the correlation between writing abilities and writing blocks appears to be, if anything, just the opposite. I should note that writing ability is probably impossible to measure in any absolute way, because manifestations of ability, like writing blocks, are largely circumstantial. An individual can be a very effective, productive writer in one circumstance and a terrible, unproductive writer in another. While many scientists (though certainly not all) hated high-school and undergraduate English classes and did poorly in them, the same people often write with fascination and skill about their own research interests. "I would have loved writing in high school," an astronomer told me, "if I could have written about subjects I really cared about." Now he can.

To the extent that poor writing results from lack of interest and attention, I should note that careless writers are rarely blocked, because their standards are usually low and blocks tend to afflict people who feel they can't meet the high standards they have set for themselves. To the extent that we can recognize differences in ability, weak, careless, awkward writers can be extremely productive even at high levels of scholarship, in any discipline, even if they have very little confidence in their ability. I know prolific scholars who rely heavily on office staff, spouses, colleagues, and editors to help them revise and polish rough, ungainly drafts.

In turn, I don't believe anyone would argue that the higher frequency of writing blocks in fields such as English and history result from weaker writing skills and motivations in these disciplines. Instead, the individually authored text holds more crucial importance, writers are more likely to work in isolation, and they are less likely to receive the kinds of support that facilitate movement through the writing process.

Regardless of your discipline, therefore, if you have entered the dissertation phase of graduate work you need to resolve the rhetorical problems that most often undermine writing at this stage:

- To make completion of the project possible, you need to identify a focused research question you can answer with authority—a question narrower than the focus of your research at large.

- If the expectations of your advisors are ambiguous or in conflict, take steps to resolve these questions, even to the point of reorganizing your graduate committee if necessary.

- If you feel that you need guidance in the writing process, remind yourself that you deserve that help and ask for it, from your advisors or from other scholars in your field.

- Find receptive, supportive readers for work in progress, among individual friends or in dissertation writing groups.

- If possible, present parts of your research findings at professional conferences or in articles. This can be extremely helpful to young scholars who doubt whether anyone is really interested in their work.

- Avoid excessive reading before and during the process of drafting chapters, especially if you find that doubts about what you are saying interrupt your work and lead you back to the library.

- Set aside blocks of time devoted to writing itself, with as little interruption as possible. In this time, keep your standards low, reminding yourself that you are free to explore the subject and revise later.

- If you find that you are stalled in the process, moving in circular loops, stop to consider what you are doing and why. Have you simply fallen into a habitual stimulus/response pattern, or are there larger rhetorical issues that need to be resolved?

Putting Writing in Its Place

It was my class who showed me that I was working in the wrong way. . . .

I learned from them that inspiration does not
come like a bolt, nor is it kinetic, energetic striv-
ing, but it comes to us slowly and all the time,
though we must regularly and every day give it a
little chance to start flowing, prime it with a little solitude and idleness. I learned that you should
feel when writing, not like Lord Byron on a moun-
taintop, but like a child stringing beads in kinder-
garten,—happy, absorbed and quietly putting one
bead on after another.

BRENDA UELAND

MAKING THE NEXT MOVE

Because the two scientists I discussed in the previous chapter were only
temporarily blocked by ambiguous relations with their advisors and other
circumstantial factors, readers might question whether they were *really*
blocked writers at all. Apart from the interdisciplinary nature of their research, no obvious factors distinguished them from the larger population
of PhD students, in their fields and others, who completed dissertations
without running into serious obstacles. When advisors clarified their expectations and helped to resolve questions of focus, these graduate students
immediately became "normal" writers, without lingering symptoms of
"writer's block."

I return to this matter of definition in order to reexamine, with specific
attention to graduate studies, the pervasive notion that writing blocks are
personal, psychological problems caused by obscure neuroses, personality
traits, or other predispositions. In earlier chapters I've argued that blocks

are instead "psychophysical" conditions manifest in particular circumstances at certain times in a writer's life. Causes and effects are difficult to distinguish, but the block arises at a specific place in the writing process, for reasons that involve particular conceptions, circumstances, and patterns of behavior. Writing blocks have emotional implications as well, no doubt related to an individual's personality, and I do not mean to exclude or trivialize these emotional factors. I simply argue that we cannot understand or resolve writing blocks by reducing them to psychological conditions or personality disorders. Because circumstances, ideas, behavior patterns, and emotions are dynamically interrelated, changes in one dimension can dramatically alter the other dimensions as well. These two scientists did not represent a personality type. Their temperaments were very different from one another, and neither was unusually inclined toward anxiety, perfectionism, insecurity, or other traits popularly associated with writing blocks. I have known many writers with those tendencies who were not blocked; yet at a particular stage of their work these two writers were.

In this period they were also anxious, insecure, and somewhat depressed, and superficial observation at that time might have suggested that these conditions represented their personalities. One of them also told me he thought he was a poor writer, even though later work demonstrated that he was not. Both had begun to question the potential value of their research, and if they had failed to produce focused accounts of it, scholars in their fields might have concluded that they were only marginally competent scientists, unfit for highly competitive research grants and positions.

The kinds of people they appeared to be therefore resulted from the complex interplay of conceptual, emotional, and circumstantial factors that all changed dramatically when they resolved the rhetorical problems that most directly caused their writing blocks. During the months prior to this resolution they were both working very hard in relative isolation and becoming increasingly distressed by their lack of progress. Partly because they were capable writers and conscientious students, they felt that they should be able to resolve these rhetorical issues on their own if they were only a bit smarter, or worked a bit harder and longer. Their inability to do so undermined their confidence as scholars and writers, along with their enjoyment in their work, and when I first talked with them I might have concluded from their discouragement that they were not sufficiently motivated to pursue advanced studies in their fields.

With experience, however, I've learned not to jump to general conclusions about individuals from the symptoms of their immediate problems. Nor can I safely assume that any one feature of a writing block represents its true and only cause. People who are having trouble with writing receive a lot of well-intentioned but useless advice from friends and advisors who assume that the solution to the problem lies in removing its most obvious manifestation. And this tendency applies to most interpersonal relations. When people seem agitated, our first reaction is to say *Just calm down.* If they seem depressed, we say, *Cheer up!* If they lack confidence, we say, *Come on! You can Do it!* If they are exhausted we say, *Just get some rest.* I have known blocked writers who suffered from stress-induced rashes, nervous tics, and chronic fatigue, and others whose professional or personal lives were in turmoil for reasons that were probably related to their writing difficulties. Most of these people had already consulted physicians, psychiatrists, or family counselors for help with these problems. But they came to me for help with their writing problems

In our meetings, therefore, my main goal is to help these writers figure out *what they need to do next*, with recognition that this probably needs to be different from what they have been doing thus far. This emphasis on action acknowledges that writing blocks are manifest in patterns of behavior that have usually become habitual, repetitive. Because we know that these movements within and around the writing process have stopped carrying the project forward, it seems sensible to consider what a different, strategically promising move might be. Because scholars tend to view writing primarily as a mental activity, they are often inattentive to what they are actually doing, and where, and for how long. They want to tell me what they have been reading and thinking, or thinking about doing, or thinking about writing, or thinking about their difficulties. They tend to describe themselves as disembodied writers whose minds have been moving through intangible intellectual terrain. All of this is interesting, but I also want to know where their bodies have been moving: exactly how they have been spending their time, and what they have *not* been doing as well.

Toward this collaborative plotting of the next move, emotional dimensions of the problem can offer valuable clues. In our first meetings, both of these graduate students in the sciences were resigned to the necessity of struggling with their projects without help, and when they described their efforts they seemed discouraged, exhausted, and vulnerable. Simply continuing these struggles did not seem useful.

When they talked about their graduate committees, however, their moods and appearances changed. The surface of weary resignation broke to reveal anger at the negligence of their advisors. They obviously felt very strongly that they needed and deserved help they were not receiving. The neuroscientist also felt injured and rejected by an advisor he had considered a close research colleague, and progress with his work was further hampered by disillusionment. When they expressed this anger and disappointment, both of these writers seemed more lively, focused, and strong, and I felt we were talking about the heart of the matter. Movement in that direction therefore seemed most promising. Even if new efforts to get attentive guidance from their advisors had failed, some of the ambiguity of their positions would have been removed. They would know more clearly where they stood, and we could talk about what they should do next.

Our goal, then, is to identify changes that remove obstacles to movement through the writing process. When they make these changes in a productive direction, writers sense to varying degrees a release into motion, at once mental and physical.

SYNTACTIC BLOCK

Many kinds of change can stimulate this release. An example of a more severely blocked writer will illustrate the ways in which a very small step in a new direction can set off a complex chain of behavioral, emotional, rhetorical, and interpersonal transformations in the writer's life.

When I first met Andrea she had completed extensive field research and reading, but she could not make a single coherent statement about her dissertation topic, even in conversation, and a two-page prospectus for her advisor was long overdue. Every point of departure, it seemed, reminded her of several other dimensions of her project, other ways of starting out, other things she needed to say first. Because Andrea was studying current political and environmental issues, events relevant to her research occurred almost daily, adding new pieces to a puzzle that was continually expanding and changing shape. When I asked her to describe her research, therefore, Andrea resorted to complex diagrams composed of circles and boxes connected by intricate networks of lines. How could a sequence of words and sentences describe such a maze of associated factors?

In her rich, inquisitive imagination, Andrea's dissertation topic had grown beyond the linear dimension of English syntax. "What I want to write about," she exclaimed one day in frustration, "is The Whole Elephant! But when I try to write I'm just describing the end of the trunk, or the tail, or a foot. You can't see the whole beast."

I asked Andrea to explain where she stood in relation to this project. How did she include herself, as a scholar and writer? Abandoning disjointed attempts to answer this question, she produced another diagram: a tiny circle in the center of a very large one. "This is me," she said, pointing to the little circle, "and this [pointing to the large one] is my dissertation topic."

This simple drawing helped me to understand what makes writing seem impossible for many scholars and difficult, to varying degrees, for anyone who attempts to write "within" a field of study. How can we write coherently, or with authority, about something that dwarfs us? Andrea's diagram also allowed me to visualize both why academic writers revert to further preparations for writing and why these loops, intended to make writing easier, usually have the opposite effect. Andrea's attempts to write made her feel that her understanding of the subject was inadequate, so she read and thought more about it. All of this time, thought, and effort simply expanded the dimensions of her research while diminishing her capacity to write about this research.

Other graduate students have elaborated this diagram with more concentric circles. Their dissertation topics, they observe, are circumscribed by their broader fields of study, within the university curriculum, within the world at large.

Writers who describe their work in this way feel not only trapped within their own fields of research but also cut off from other people, activities, and interests. In this diagram, where would you put friends, lovers, relatives, or children? A cat or a goldfish might be content to occupy this space, but it isn't much fun, as a rule, to inhabit someone else's field of scholarship, even if you have similar interests. I've known scholars who were so absorbed in specialized research that the world in which other people live had become both an abstraction and a potential *dis*traction from the kind of concentration they considered essential to real scholarship. "I feel like I'm sliding into a deep hole," a first-year graduate student in chemistry once told me, "and when I get to the bottom, where I need to be if I'm going to be a real chemist, I won't be able to see anything else."

What's wrong with this picture? How can young scholars become experts and authoritative writers in a field without becoming absorbed in it? What are the alternatives to the idea that one must become immersed *in* a field of study in order to write *about* it? Isn't this the unavoidable condition of life for the dedicated, successful scholar?

This idea of "immersion" reminds me again of Stafford's image of the swimmer. A lake is indeed bigger, deeper, than anyone who might enter it—large enough to drown in if we become overwhelmed by it, rigid, motionless, immersed. So is a field of study if we think of it as a whole body of knowledge, writing, and thought. Individuals can't consume or encompass all of that material, and in the effort to do so they will surely drown.

But language, like water, is also a buoyant medium in which writers can float and move, with "little strokes against the material nearest them," if they "reach out with ease and confidence." A lake might be something big to drown in, but water is a substance of our own gravity and constitution—something we are made of. So is language. And using the medium of language in the activity of writing is something we can always do.

The fundamental misconception that paralyzed Andrea, as it does many other writers, was the idea that her field of research represented her dissertation: the task of writing and the thing to be written. Actually, a dissertation isn't anything until it is written; and it will never become anything except through the activity of writing: those little strokes in the medium of language. Writing is a particular kind of embodied, generative, constructive activity through which things like dissertations come about. And if we are not directly engaged in this activity for sustained periods of time, such things will never come about.

If you are actually engaged in this activity, at any moment you are not doing anything so grand as producing a whole dissertation in a whole field of research. You are just constructing or reconstructing a sentence in the little space before you, coordinating language and thought for that purpose. So it is with any complex project. If you are actually building a house, not just planning to build one, at any moment you will actually be doing something more specific: pouring concrete into forms, cutting boards, hammering nails, soldering pipes, or painting walls. The whole project will turn out best if you pay attention to this activity. You will need plans, of course, and will pause from time to time to think about what you are doing. But thinking about building a house will not get a house built. Recipes and raw materials for an elaborate meal will not satisfy anyone's appetite. And Andrea's elaborate ideas and schematic diagrams about her dissertation were not substantial enough to satisfy her advisor, who had withheld help, he said, "until you get something written."

"The task at hand," I told Andrea, "has to be littler than you are—one of the things you are doing in your life—or it won't be something you can do." I tried to draw a new diagram of my own, in which her dissertation project was a little circle among others in the larger circle of her life, within the still larger world in which she lived. "There has to be space and time in your life for other people, other activities and interests, and then some blocks of time for working on this writing project."

My diagram got the point made, but it wasn't quite accurate, other students have since told me. The kind of arrangement they would like to achieve, a couple of them said, is composed of overlapping spheres. Their disciplines, relationships, and other interests are partly in and partly outside their lives, within the world at large, and so is their own research topic.

In the midst of these overlapping spheres, writing simply requires some time and space, devoted to the activity of composing sentences. People who feel blocked are, for a variety of reasons, not clearing that time and space in their lives, or do not use it to compose sentences. They are always doing something else that seems, at the moment, more important.

In Andrea's case, the initial release into motion resulted from my own frustration, as I listened to sentences that began, "Well, I think what I mean is that . . . " and then dissolved into retractions, diversions, qualifications, and ultimately diagrams.

"Just complete your sentence," I finally said. "Start over until you get it finished. I don't care how long it takes."

So we worked on that sentence for several minutes, stopping each time the structure broke or became entangled, going back to the beginning that I had written down and adding another phrase, until we had a complete, direct statement about her research.

The construction of that sentence untangled something I still don't fully understand, but the effects were obvious. Previously tense, pale, and solemn, Andrea flushed with pleasure, began to laugh, and became very lively, as though moving blood and oxygen had broken through some restriction.

"Now just keep writing sentences in the same patient fashion," I suggested, "without letting them break apart." Over the following weekend Andrea filled two pages with sentences about her research and gave them to her advisor. With this document in hand, he acknowledged the value of her work and began to give her the support she needed from him. In subsequent weeks he collaborated with Andrea on a professional article. She also began to complete drafts of her dissertation chapters and eventually received a postdoctoral fellowship for a proposal she had written in one weekend, just before the deadline. About six months after she completed that first sentence she had finished and successfully defended a full draft of her dissertation.

I used the term "syntactic block" for this kind of interference with writing ability because in the act of writing, thought and language converge in the unfolding syntax of sentences, much as they do in speech. Whatever we say in writing must be possible to say in a linear sequence of words and sentences. Ideas and understandings can take other forms, including nonlinguistic, nonlinear ones. Some of them can be represented—with diagrams, graphs, mathematical equations, or paintings—and others cannot.

We can sense, or imagine, all sorts of connections, distinctions, patterns, and layers of meaning that do not lend themselves to the structure of language. I'm sure that "The Whole Elephant" Andrea wanted to write about had taken shape in her agile mind, but the whole intricate form of that understanding could not be bound to strings of words or, for that matter, to any other medium of representation.

Popular psychology attributes these holistic, graphic, intuitive ways of thinking to the "right brain" and linear, analytical, linguistic thinking to the "left brain." In a book based on these distinctions, *Writing the Natural Way*, Gabriele Rico argues that traditional methods of teaching writing limit our natural powers of expression by confining the use of written language to left brain sequences, rules, and mechanical procedures. Rico therefore advocates the use of cluster diagrams to engage the right brain and release its creative, expressive powers into the writing process. "Clustering," like freewriting, can be a useful way to generate ideas when writers feel overly cautious or dull.

Both writing and thinking can become rigidly linear, cut off from broader understandings, and individuals' minds do function differently. Scientists can often get most of what they need out of a professional article by looking at the figures or key equations, while I have to plod through the text. In a freshman course I noticed that art and architecture students tended to represent plans for their papers not in linear outlines but in the equivalent of cluster diagrams: lots of interconnected boxes or circles that indicated spatial relations among ideas. This is also the way Andrea tried to explain what her dissertation was about, when language failed.

But those art and architecture students often had considerable difficulty transferring their two-dimensional, visual conceptions to the linear form of an essay, and doing so usually required another step, closer to an outline or list. To make progress with her dissertation, Andrea certainly didn't need to practice "clustering." This is what she was already doing, and in some ways her writing block resulted from her effort to make language represent those complicated clusters of related ideas. Because this was impossible, she spoke in fragments and became, as a writer, altogether mute.

Andrea could not get anywhere with this project until she surrendered to the fact that a dissertation is the thing *written*, not just imagined, and that imagination, insight, understanding must develop through that medium. The medium of written language holds considerable power to represent not just strings of information, but also arrangements of ideas, layers of meaning, and hierarchies of importance. We can discover and use that power, however, only within the structure of language itself, which is just as "natural" as any other medium of thought and expression.

SETTLING FOR LESS

You might assume that after months of frustration and anxiety over work that was going nowhere, Andrea would be elated by her rapid progress. She was certainly relieved, and the momentum she gained in her writing set other parts of her life into motion as well: a postdoctoral fellowship and then a teaching job, publications, conferences, and a widening network of contacts with scholars and organizations in her field. When she began to complete and release her writing, Andrea stepped out of isolation into a stimulating world of interaction and communication. Ironically, when nothing was happening Andrea had seemed exhausted by her efforts to do the impossible. In the flurry of activity that surrounded her completion of writing projects she was much more relaxed and alert.

It is important to recognize, however, that movement beyond a writing block can result in feelings of disillusionment and letdown. The patterns of behavior, ideas, efforts, and expectations that contribute to a writing block have often become strongly habitual and familiar, even comfortable. Letting go of them can therefore produce a sense of loss. The person who now writes with relative ease is somewhat different from the one who could not write, and this transition bears costs as well as benefits.

A sense of disillusionment and loss often results from the lowering of standards. When Andrea and I reduced her ideas about her dissertation to a single coherent sentence—something communicable—we also stripped away most of the labyrinthine complexities that made thinking about the subject so interesting to her. Putting her ideas into a linear sequence of sentences also concretized and therefore limited these ideas to a single rendition, while the real issues, events, and perspectives she studied were constantly changing. The writing she produced was much less, in this respect, than her understanding of the subject, her thoughts about writing, her idealized conception of a dissertation that could represent "The Whole Elephant." As chapters and passages of a real dissertation emerged, they introduced and pursued only one line of inquiry, with a limited review of the relevant literature and a focused sequence of arguments that included only a small proportion of her research material.

When she entered my office and tossed the latest chapter on my desk one day, Andrea said with a dismissive laugh, "Well, here it is. Anything worth doing is worth doing badly." When the postdoctoral fellowship application she had thrown together just before the deadline was accepted, she expressed disbelief that the standards for acceptance were "so low." To continue writing productively, Andrea had to accept lower standards for performance, both in her own work and in her conception of the discipline she entered, now as a participating member. I've met several graduate students who were simply unwilling to make this sacrifice, even when they understood the consequences.

In other words, writers are often heavily invested in the way of thinking, working, and living in which a block is embedded. And because these investments are understandable (though perhaps unsustainable and ultimately impractical) we can't simply dismiss them. The dissertation phase of graduate work is transitory and often impoverished, but it offers certain kinds of freedom, safety, and intellectual stimulation that can become very attractive in comparison with the uncertainties, responsibilities, and necessary changes that lie beyond the completion of a PhD. Moving beyond a writing block, one must contend with job searches and interviews, publishers, relocations, and colleagues in professional communities. Publication exposes writers to all sorts of potential misunderstandings, factional conflicts, and uncomfortable alliances that sully a pure, contemplative appreciation for the intellectual depth and complexity of a discipline—the qualities that initially attract many students to academic careers.

This is why Carl identified with the rabbit in my analogy. If he pursued one line of inquiry, one clear argument, his thesis would pin him down. Other scholars could then locate his position, and although he was entirely capable of sustaining cohesive arguments in writing, he did not feel ready to identify himself with specific factions in his discipline. Any single thesis would misrepresent the breadth of his interests and might launch his career in a direction he was not prepared to choose. This is one reason for which graduate students often confuse the dissertation with their entire field of study. What they are trying to write, then, is not a "thesis" but the whole frame of reference for their careers as scholars. Because any single line of inquiry would misrepresent that career potential, continuing to write from a specific viewpoint requires a willingness to settle for less than you feel capable of understanding.

This potential dissatisfaction extends also to writing style. When our thoughts on a subject are congested and the process of composing sentences is frequently interrupted, the sentences we write tend to become congested as well, because we are laboriously attempting to represent our complex thinking *about* what we are trying to write. When we are writing directly on a train of thought, by contrast, sentences usually have a more open, linear flow, and they connect more directly with one another in passages. To the reader, the writing seems more accessible and clear because it is easier to follow, and it is easier to follow because it is saying something directly, not trying to say everything.

As readers, almost all of us appreciate accessible, relaxed, fluent writing. As writers, however, scholars often feel that their work should also be deep and complex, and writing that is extremely easy to follow can seem too simple. I once spent about thirty minutes helping a graduate student in the history of art rewrite one long, convoluted, impenetrable sentence from the theory chapter of her dissertation. As we deleted and condensed phrases, restructured the sentence, and eventually reduced it to a third of its original length, I continually asked the student if a specific change would improve the sentence and retain her meaning, and in each case she said that it would. When we were finished and read the sentence aloud, however, she looked dissatisfied. "What's wrong with it?" I asked.

She hesitated to admit what was wrong, and then said, "It's too easy to understand . . . too obvious. I mean, is this all I'm saying? It doesn't sound important at all. It doesn't sound like a dissertation."

I reminded her that it was her sentence and her dissertation, not mine. Although this was probably the clearest way to make her point, she was free to make it less clear if she felt it was too simple. And that is what she chose to do. She restored some of the phrasing we had removed to make the sentence a bit more convoluted and complex.

Writers who are accustomed to difficulty are especially vulnerable to this perception that whatever they can say easily and clearly is too obvious, too simple, insufficiently deep and important. The fact that they can say something without difficulty suggests to them that this cannot be the *real* point they have to make. Further thinking and further reading might transport them to the next level of understanding, sufficiently difficult to grasp to represent real scholarship. When I was caught up in this struggle to write beyond my own level of comprehension, the advisor who had helped me get my topic in focus ended the struggle with a blunt remark: "Only a fool tries to express the ineffable. Just write about what you know."

How did Andrea manage to settle for less and write so quickly, even though she felt that she was producing work of very low quality? What kept her going once she had produced that first sentence?

Three factors kept her moving:

1. She continually reminded herself that while she was writing she was an unreliable judge of her work. Instead, she just "made a pile of pages," she said, without trying to assess their worth.

2. Other readers—including advisors, friends, and a granting agency—seemed to think her writing was interesting and clear, even when she produced it very quickly. From this reception she concluded that either her perceptions were false or their standards were much lower than she had imagined. But either conclusion favored rapid production.

3. Above all, Andrea enjoyed the sensation of release and movement: the feeling of language and thought converging directly into a flow of sentences. Both her mind and her body told her that this movement was more wholesome and pleasurable than disembodied thought, linguistic paralysis, the stillness of held breath.

GENDER, TIME, AND SPACE

About 75 percent of the people who come to me for help with obstacles in the writing process are women, and women represent an even larger proportion of those who continue to meet with me until the problem is resolved. These differences are about the same for students who work with my colleague, Barbara LeGendre.

We might conclude from this imbalance that women are most vulnerable to writing blocks and their causes, but anecdotal evidence suggests that this conclusion is false. When people mention colleagues, students, or friends who are struggling unsuccessfully with writing projects, these subjects of hearsay are as often as not men. If the frequency of blocking does differ slightly between men and women, in one direction or the other, the difference remains irrelevant to individuals and to my work with them.

The most plausible explanation for the disproportion among my students is that women are more likely to seek and accept help when they are in trouble or, by inversion, that men are reluctant to ask for help in the same circumstances. In her essay "Anxious Writers in Context: Graduate School and Beyond," Lynn Z. Bloom cites research findings that women are *not* more prone to anxiety about writing, but that "women are more oriented than men toward preventing and relieving medical and psychological problems."

If these observations are valid, larger numbers of men are struggling with writing problems in isolation, and are therefore more likely to fail academically before they request help with these problems. Citing other research, Bloom suggests that women might be more vulnerable to "the pressures of writing a dissertation" because they "in general have lower self-confidence than men." We could reason that this insecurity makes women more likely to seek help with their writing, but we could argue the reverse just as plausibly: that women are perceived to lack confidence, and are perhaps believed to have more trouble, because they are more willing to ask for help when they face difficulty. Perhaps rather than having lower confidence they simply have better sense.

In her study of undergraduates working on senior projects at Miami University, Mary Kupiec Cayton observed that roughly equal proportions of men and women enountered writing blocks, but that they described and perhaps experienced these problems very differently. The men in Cayton's study tended to attribute their difficulties to problems of writing strategy, competing priorities, and lack of motivation. The women were inclined to describe problems of developing appropriate voice and authority in relation to the audience, with emphasis on the emotional and interpersonal dimensions of their experience. Cayton found these women more vulnerable to responses from advisors and peers, and she suggested that they still have more difficulty finding a clear, secure identity in academic communities. She acknowledged, however, that these seniors did not represent the student population at large and that significant questions of interpretation remain. Men and women might choose different ways of describing the same problem, revealing or masking certain dimensions, and in any case the study offers no clear definition of the "blocks" these students were describing. The fact that "most described at least one major occasion of blocking during the course of their projects" suggests that the "blocks" under investigation represented a variety of problems.

All of these questions remain open, however, because professional help with writing blocks is so rarely available, especially to writers at advanced levels of higher education. Men or women have little reason to look for this help if there is no evidence that it exists, and we have no idea how many try to find assistance without success.

Setting predispositions aside, it remains possible that the *circumstantial* causes of writing blocks are sometimes linked with gender. If women are more insecure about their positions as scholars and writers, perhaps their positions are actually less secure in some cases. In numbers and in status, men dominate many academic disciplines, and when women feel that male faculty members do not take their work seriously, sometimes they are right. And if they seem to need more guidance and attention, perhaps they are receiving too little. Before Andrea suggested to her advisor that they should coauthor a paper on their collaborative work, he had coauthored articles only with male graduate students. In the sciences and some of the social sciences, women are a minority among graduate students and a much smaller minority among faculty. Their graduate committees are often composed entirely of men, and as assistant professors untenured women are sometimes the only women in a department's faculty. Whether their insecurities are real or imagined, the circumstances that add to the "pressures of writing a dissertation" or of publication can be very real. Like representatives of other minorities, women often feel they must try harder to achieve status and respect equal to that of male peers, and trying harder rarely makes a task easier.

Factors of time and space can also differ for women writers. Books and articles on writing blocks almost always mention Tillie Olsen's *Silences* and Virginia Woolf's *A Room of One's Own*, which underscore the difficulty—even the impossibility—of writing when you cannot find space and time in your life. "Few have been the writer-women," Tillie Olsen observes

> who have had George Eliot's luck of "the perfect happiness of living with a being who protects and stimulates in me the health of highest productivity,"—but the writer-men in such circumstances are and have been many. And not only wives: mothers, sisters, daughters, lovers, helper women, secretaries, housekeepers, watchers and warders.

The problem of establishing a role for oneself as a writer among the competing roles of parent, spouse, housekeeper, taxi service, or employee certainly has not vanished in the decades since Woolf and Olsen wrote. Men are simply more likely to face the challenges of juggling these roles, and women in graduate studies or professions are more likely to have equal time, space, and independence to pursue their careers. I have known several men who were struggling to complete dissertations or publications while sharing responsibilities for child care, cooking, and housework, or holding part-time jobs, and many of the women who encounter blocks have ample time and space for writing. Their difficulties have nothing to do with responsibilities unevenly borne by women.

Satisfying, supportive relationships of all kinds can help writers to keep their work in perspective, and the idea that marriages, children, and other commitments make writers less productive is, as a generalization, false. Women and men who have too little going on in their lives beyond their scholarship sometimes have the most trouble writing productively. Reading, thinking, and other preparations for writing the hypothetical dissertation or book come to define the writer's existence, to the extent that real writing can never live up to the abstract conception. The absence of relationships and responsibilities can inflate the importance of writing in ways that intensify the pressure to perform. I knew a PhD student whose husband had taken a job in another state and took their child with him, to give her complete freedom from distraction for finishing her dissertation. But this luxury became a curse. Living alone in a student apartment, cut off from her family, she was terribly lonely, and every week she spent trying to write made her feel more guilty and discouraged. She was completely absorbed in a world of ideas that represented everything absent from her life, and she could not write productively until a generous advisor, who recognized the nature of the problem, provided some of the real human contact and attention this writer had sacrificed to her work.

Nonetheless, women still represent the great majority of single parents, and when both spouses have full-time jobs or educational commitments, women still, on average, spend the most time maintaining the household and caring for children. Women are also more likely to make career sacrifices when the demands of the partners' careers are in conflict.

For example "Ellen," one of two case studies in Bloom's essay (mentioned above), could find neither space nor time in her marriage to complete her graduate work. When she began her doctoral studies in philosophy, Ellen's husband, "Stan," received an assistant professorship in history that assumed priority over Ellen's research and writing.

> Their family pattern called for Ellen to do nearly all the housework and to care for their two young children herself, generally unrelieved by Stan or a sitter. When the children were awake, they dominated the apartment and eliminated both the temporal and physical contexts conducive to writing. Ellen, temperamentally most alert in the morning, had no choice but to do most of her reading and writing at night after the children were in bed, when she was tired. Her family situation and her academic situation continually impinged on each other.

Ellen's situation worsened when her husband moved to another academic job and place, because he had failed to complete a book essential to tenure, and Ellen was cut off from the direct supports of her graduate program. Her research and writing slid further into subordination to family priorities, and in her fragmented preparations to write, "every topic suggested a myriad of others." Because both partners were blocked writers in competing careers, they could not help each other with their difficulties or even talk about their work without conflict. In the four years after Bloom met her, in a workshop on writing anxiety, Ellen had not completed a single chapter, and unless circumstances changed dramatically she was not likely ever to do so.

The pressures on "Sarah," the other case in Bloom's essay, were not obviously linked with gender roles, but they underscore the difficulties of writing against competing demands on our time. Sarah had completed and even published parts of her dissertation when she became an assistant professor at a major university. Teaching and other faculty responsibilities then continually put her dissertation on the back burner. She could not bring it forward as a priority until her university told her that she would lose her job if she did not complete her PhD. With her confidence lowered by pressure, Sarah fell prey to performance anxiety and excessively high standards that threw her continually into prewriting activity. With Bloom's help and support from a dissertation writing group, Sarah resolved these problems, created blocks of time for writing, and completed her PhD before the deadline.

Scholars like Sarah who accept teaching jobs before they complete the PhD enter another hazardously liminal condition: that of becoming a professor while remaining, in some respects, a graduate student. In these circumstances the role of professor is almost invariably more compelling, and more immediately demanding, than the roles of graduate student and dissertation writer, even when there are looming consequences that should compel one to write. In Sarah's case, Bloom notes, "there was far more pressure from her chairman, peers, and students to function fully in her teaching role at the expense of her graduate work." Every graduate student I have known in this situation has had to struggle, some desperately and unsuccessfully, to find time and attention for writing. And while completion of the PhD has become increasingly essential for tenure-track positions, growing numbers of adjunct positions have drawn PhD candidates into demanding teaching jobs before they finish their dissertations. In many cases these positions do not impose deadlines for completion of the PhD, and degree candidates in these circumstance are even more likely to postpone writing until the project withers from neglect.

All of these cases underscore a basic requirement for writing anything long and complex. To make substantial progress, writers need to spend blocks of time *actually writing*, and these periods of writing need to be linked in close sequence. Otherwise, you will lose whatever trail you blaze in a thicket of distractions and competing priorities, and when you return to the work you will spend much of your time trying to restore your concentration and to remember the direction your work was taking. "An important step in becoming a writer," Victoria Nelson says in her book *On Writer's Block*, "is learning how to allocate *time* in your life for writing. Misuse of time is more likely to inhibit writing than any other factor." It is virtually impossible to write productively when time fully devoted to this work is fragmented or sparse.

We have considered cases in which family responsibilities, other social commitments, and demanding jobs make finding adequate time and space for writing extremely difficult. Ellen's writing project was essentially in checkmate: continually pushed into submissive positions in which movement was impossible. Women who return to graduate studies as single parents, or as wives of men with established careers, often feel that long delays in their writing result from their own lack of knowledge or ability. When I ask direct questions about their work schedules, however, it becomes obvious that their writing suffers from a shortage of time and sustained attention. They are trying to write (or more often preparing to write) in the scattered pieces of time left over when their other numerous responsibilities have been met. In those stolen moments they are often exhausted and distracted, yet they feel that they must put that precious time to great use, and when little comes of it they feel guilty and discouraged.

Understanding the real nature of the problem can at least help to restore lost confidence, and when they recognize their actual needs as writers, some of these women can reorganize their lives to the extent that they clear regular periods of time for their work. It is better to establish two to four uninterrupted hours at regular intervals than to find whole days more widely and erratically spaced. We can't expect to write productively for eight or ten hours at a time, and maintaining voice and continuity requires closely sequenced writing sessions.

Bloom's case studies, my own, and other accounts of writing practices suggest that for most serious writers, whether they are women or men, there are four contextual requirements for productivity:

1. *Make writing a clear priority in your life.*

Writing doesn't have to be the highest priority in your life, and it probably shouldn't be. But it does need to be *a* priority that deserves sustained attention for certain periods of most days each week.

If you are supposed to be working on a dissertation, therefore, writing is your job. It doesn't have to be your favorite job or the most important thing you do. But if you want to get through graduate school and move on with the rest of your life, it is a job that has to be done, and like other jobs it requires physical presence and concentration for substantial portions of your time. Writing a dissertation isn't just an intellectual endeavor. This text will not miraculously emerge from your thoughts while you are doing other things.

2. *Set aside times for writing when you are most relaxed and alert.*

The times people choose for writing are often vestiges of old habits and time constraints. Undergraduates tend to write in the evening or late at night because they have classes and other responsibilities during the day. But habits of nocturnal writing often persist, unexamined, long after the writer's circumstances have changed, among people who really function best in the morning. The majority of professional writers prefer to work during the day.

Regardless of your preferences, this needs to be a matter of choice, to the extent that you can choose times for writing. After all, you probably schedule other activities at appropriate times, according to your needs. I imagine that you cook or buy meals when you are likely to be hungry, that you sleep when you are tired, and that you run or play tennis when you have some energy, not when you are completely exhausted. Yet a surprising number of people try to write when they are least rested and alert, or most likely to be distracted.

3. *Find a particular place for writing.*

Ellen had no place, in her apartment or elsewhere, designated for her writing, and this was one of the main reasons for which writing never happened. This need for "a room of one's own" is a common problem for dissertation writers. Because they rarely have private offices and sometimes share small apartments, advanced graduate students often become, like undergraduates, itinerant writers who carry portions of their dissertation materials from one place to another, losing time in transit and in the difficulty of restoring concentration. A couple of blocked writers I worked with were constantly trying to find the best place for writing that day, moving their projects from their apartments to the library, a shared office, a public computer facility, or a café. The material they needed was often somewhere else, and each place affected them differently, making it difficult to sustain continuity.

If you do not have the luxury of an office or study equipped with your own computer, where you can keep all of your material together undisturbed, you might be able to find specific places where you can write regularly with a reasonable amount of comfort. Some people find this easier than others, due to their dispositions, and preferences vary radically. I can't imagine how my students write papers in crowded computer facilities, or against the background of loud music in their rooms. Yet I composed much of my dissertation by hand in a law school cafeteria where I didn't know anyone and could spend hours undisturbed, looking up to watch people or stare out the broad windows when I needed to rest my eyes and brain. Some people would find that public setting for writing intolerable.

4. Dedicate this time and place to actual writing.

Although available time and space are necessities for most productive writers, they are not in themselves sufficient to bring writing about; nor do they necessarily prevent writing blocks. I have known a number of blocked writers who had plenty of time available for writing and private offices or rooms where they could concentrate on their work. Yet they were not actually writing. Some spent enormous amounts of time, like Bonnie Friedman, "killing flies": continually reorganizing their work spaces, materials, and plans in endless preparation for writing. Others seemed too paralyzed by the emptiness of that time and space to fill it with words on the page, or were continually drawn away from it by a restless need to do something "real."

But writing is, as I've argued throughout this book, a real physical activity of letting language and thought converge in sentences on a page or screen, through motions of our arms, hands, and eyes, with our bodies present in a time and place. It is not just a work of the imagination. You are either doing it or you are not, and are instead doing something else. Writing is, as I told Carl, a little fire you tend regularly, with sustained attention, patience, and acceptance. It doesn't have to be so dramatic as a bonfire and perhaps can't be for any length of time. The main requirement is that you have to be there and to keep it going: word after word, sentence after sentence, page after page.

eight

Scholarly Production

How is the world of scholarship organized, and what part does writing and publishing play in it? What part do you want to play in it, and how will the way you write and publish affect whether you can play the part you have chosen? Good questions, for which, not surprisingly, there are no solid answers. Not surprisingly, because academics are as unwilling as others to study the organization of their social world. They don't want their secrets exposed or their favorite myths revealed as fairy tales.

HOWARD BECKER

SYNOPSIS

Thus far I've suggested that in academic work writing blocks become increasingly common at higher levels of scholarship, especially in fields where the written text represents the primary locus of knowledge and medium of performance. Junior and senior undergraduates are therefore more likely to encounter writing blocks than are freshmen. Writing blocks are more common among graduate students than among undergraduates; and graduate students most often become mired in the writing process in the last stage of their studies, when they are writing dissertations or master's theses. At each of these levels severe writing difficulties are most common in the humanities and in qualitative branches of the social sciences, where the individually authored text assumes vital importance.

I also argued that professionals in rhetoric and composition have largely ignored writing blocks because writing programs are usually based on the opposite premise: that difficulties with writing are most common at the lowest stratum of the academic world, among college freshmen. As students gain knowledge and experience, moving up through undergraduate and graduate studies into professions, they should (according to this premise) need less help with writing. Although freshmen are inexperienced writers who both need and deserve instruction to adapt their skills to assignments in college courses, in fact they rarely become lost or bogged down in the process of completing these assignments. As a consequence, composition teachers seldom observe serious writing blocks, which tend to occur beyond the levels at which help with writing is readily available.

How can we account for these conflicting premises: that people at the bottom or at the top of academic hierarchies have the most serious difficulties with writing?

We are obviously referring to somewhat different kinds of difficulty, though the contrasts are not as sharp as we might suppose. Because college freshmen typically lack knowledge and experience of some fairly basic requirements of academic writing, much of the instruction they need is more or less "mechanical." For example, they often need review of grammar and punctuation to reduce error, along with instruction in the use of quotations and citation. They need help moving beyond the simplistic template of the "five-paragraph theme" taught in many high schools, toward more complex, sophisticated arguments based on readings. They should also learn how to read their own work and that of other writers critically and analytically. It is generally true that writers at advanced levels of the university no longer need instruction in these "basic skills," and no longer experience these types of difficulty.

I have also noted, however, that writing blocks tend to occur in periods of transition, when stakes and standards rise, tasks become more complex, and established methods no longer work. In this respect college freshmen run into difficulties very similar to those at higher levels of scholarship. The efforts of college freshmen to devise new methods for meeting unfamiliar demands do not usually lead to writing blocks, partly because new students receive lots of instruction through this transition. Although the assignments they complete are somewhat longer and more complex than those in high school, and the standards for performance are somewhat higher, the great majority of undergraduates can continue to complete these assignments in one draft, often in a single session of composing. As a consequence, they can usually avoid the messy loops of rethinking and revising in which blocked writers become trapped. When we encourage undergraduates to look more deeply into the topic, read their own work critically, avoid settling for their first thoughts, and revise their papers, we are steering them not only toward better writing but also toward new kinds of writing difficulties that few of them have ever experienced.

Although writing programs are built on the premise that entering students have the most trouble with writing and need the most instruction, few composition teachers would argue that writing gets *easier* as we move through higher levels of instruction and scholarship. We would have to be blind and deaf to ignore evidence that struggles with writing continue, change, and often intensify beyond the first years of undergraduate work. To reconcile this undeniable evidence with the notion that college freshmen have the most trouble, we conveniently assume that experienced writers need less help *contending* with difficulty. Advanced degrees carry the questionable assumption that certified scholars have also learned what they need to know about writing (and about teaching) without need for further guidance. And while we do our best to make writing easier for college freshmen (who often assume, therefore, that good writers are people who write easily), beyond that level writing difficulties of all kinds, avoidable and unavoidable, are accepted, concealed, or attributed to personal weakness.

A HIDDEN CATEGORY

If the pattern of frequency I have proposed holds true, we should expect that struggles within the writing process will continue to intensify as people move from PhD programs into faculty positions as assistant professors, then into tenured positions and further promotions. If you are struggling to complete a dissertation, in other words, completion of your PhD might not bring the relief you had hoped for. Perhaps at the end of this long, disorienting tunnel there is no light, but another tunnel, even darker and more convoluted than the last.

Before we consider this gloomy hypothesis I must confess that we cannot really test it. Understanding the nature of these problems allows us to make some educated guesses about their occurrence in academic professions, but there is very little direct evidence to suggest how frequently scholars become derailed in the writing process or exactly why this happens when it does.

If graduate students are reluctant to admit that they are struggling with writing projects, for fear of revealing weakness, faculty members are less likely to do so. And because "writing" at most universities is something people in English teach to freshmen, professors have even less reason to imagine that anyone could help them with highly specialized books and articles. Interdisciplinary writing programs sometimes organize faculty workshops on teaching that include discussion of professional writing practices, but I don't know of any university that offers direct help to professors with writing problems.

Occasionally I hear about professors who can't get manuscripts done, and everyone in a large university knows people who were denied tenure because they did not publish. Now and then faculty members tell me that they have been meaning to schedule a meeting to talk about their writing problems, but these meetings rarely occur and when they do they are not always about writing blocks per se. In some cases, including a college dean and senior professors, individuals were simply dissatisfied with the *kinds* of academic writing they had been doing throughout their careers and wanted to experiment with new styles and forms, for different audiences. If they had become unproductive, the main reason was that they had lost interest and pleasure in conventional scholarly writing in their fields.

Available literature on "writer's block" also contains very few references to professional academic writers. As I noted in the first chapter, self-help books on writing blocks usually emphasize forms of "expressive" writing: fiction, poetry, autobiographical work, or occasionally popular journalism. Examples of blocked or anguished writers are typically drawn from biographical and autobiographical accounts of well-known authors such as Coleridge, Wordsworth, Proust, and Flaubert who were afflicted by grave doubts, frustrations, and dry spells in their creativity (and we know of their difficulties, ironically, because they produced enough to become famous authors). These "creative blocks," as Victoria Nelson calls them, reveal some emotional, cognitive, and behavioral patterns relevant to all writers, but the rhetorical causes and implications of writing difficulties vary radically among the contexts in which individuals work. As a consequence, literary struggles to find creative energy and inspiration shed only a dim light on the problems academic writers face. Consider, for example, this advice from Anne Lamont's popular reflection on writing difficulties, *Bird by Bird*:

> Sometimes you may find it useful to let your characters huddle in the wings without you, preparing for their roles, improvising dialogue, while you set the stage for their appearance. Imagine yourself as a set designer for a play or for the movie version of the story you are working on. It may help to know what the room (or the ship or the office or the meadow) looks like where the action will be taking place. You want to know its feel, its temperature, its colors.

The "you" in this passage (and in most of Lamont's book and others of its genre) is not an assistant professor who is trying to complete a book on terrace farming in Nepal or on nutrition in American prisons while teaching two or three courses per semester. Nor is this the writer Victoria Nelson has in mind when she says, in *On Writer's Block*, "You will discover, once you begin actually writing the piece, how much closer you have moved to the mysterious living center of your story-to-be by imagining it and dwelling inside it instead of describing it from the outside looking in." Imagination and invention are not necessarily virtues for scholars who want to understand, describe, and explain the objects of their research with accuracy. In "objective" genres, authors want to remain mindful that they *are* on the "outside looking in." They are trying very hard not to drift into the invention of stories, through immersion in their own subjectivity.

The generalized, hypothetical readers these books address are instead aspiring writers of fiction or poetry who might benefit from the words and experiences of prominent novelists, poets, dramatists, and, in the case of Natalie Goldberg's *Writing Down the Bones*, Zen masters. Although scholars generate a very large proportion of the material published each year, they do not appear to represent the category of real "writers" in these books. In fact there are very few examples, apart from famous authors, of *any* real people struggling or failing or finally managing to complete particular kinds of texts in specific circumstances.

Well-known literary figures are also the subjects of some scholarly studies of writing maladies, such as Cecile Nebel's *The Dark Side of Creativity: Blocks, Unfinished Works and the Urge to Destroy* and Zachary Leader's *Writer's Block*. These literary studies do not attempt to identify causes and solutions for writing problems among professional writers in general. Like Robert Holkeboer's *Creative Agony: Why Writers Suffer*, these books examine the varieties of frustration, suffering, and self-destruction often considered to be natural dimensions of artistic creation. While traditional forms of writing instruction characterize "the writer" as a tidy, methodical person who calmly assembles cohesive essays from detailed plans constructed in outlines, we associate the production of "creative" writing with all sorts of artistic turmoil and anxiety. "Self-doubt, a sense of impotence, anguish, inadequacy, uncertainty have more often than not accompanied artistic creativity," Cecile Nebel asserts at the beginning of *The Dark Side of Creativity*, as though these afflictions were inescapable. Among them, blocks appear to be routine occupational hazards, resulting not from particular circumstances but from the artistic temperament itself, or from intense desire to be original.

Which pattern best characterizes academic authors? Do they complete their books and articles in an orderly, efficient fashion, like the Good Student? Or do they wrestle with their muses and demons in an anguished quest for excellence, like the Suffering Artist? Neither, perhaps, or either, or both. There are no comparable stereotypes of scholars as writers, whether idealized, romanticized, or agonized. There are stereotypes, largely negative, of academic writing *styles*, in publication. People associate scholarly prose with density, abstraction, and jargon. According to popular impressions, scholars inhabit their own little ivory towers, in which they write for other intellectuals in styles that general audiences find unintelligible. But we can't easily imagine what academic writers are doing in those ivory towers, behind the closed doors of their offices. Periodically books and articles "come out" in print. How they reach that point of completion remains a mystery.

Nor are there many case studies of writing problems among professors, even though we know that such problems occur. Mike Rose's edited collection of essays, *When a Writer Can't Write* (1985), is perhaps the only volume devoted primarily to blocks and anxieties in academic writing, but most of these essays concern undergraduates or writers in general. Only Lynn Z. Bloom's essay, mentioned in the previous chapter, turns attention beyond undergraduate ranks to the problems of graduate students.

BINGE WRITING VERSUS MODERATION

One exception to this rule is the work of psychologist Robert Boice, who has specialized in the study of methods and problems among professional writers, including scholars. In one of these studies, Boice tried to measure the effectiveness and effects of "binge patterns" in the writing habits of untenured professors, in comparison with writers who work at regular, moderate paces. Boice's prior contacts with hundreds of scholars led him to suspect that the majority of academic writers hold the romantic notions of "creative agony" commonly thought essential to artistic genius. These scholars believe "that binges of writing offer special advantages, including loosened, brilliant thinking and rare opportunities for quick, efficient completions of overdue projects." From his perspective as a psychologist, Boice described these binges as periods of "creative illness"—conditions of hypomania, characterized by heightened emotions and passionate engagement in the task, followed by periods of exhaustion, depression, and blocking. A large proportion of academic writers, Boice claims, view manic immersion in a writing project as the necessary condition for productivity and creative thinking.

To test this popular theory, Boice closely studied the writing activities of sixteen untenured professors from a variety of disciplines, over a period of two years. Eight of these scholars were confirmed "binge writers" who described their methods as "highly euphoric and essential to their best, most brilliant writing." The other eight had established routine, moderate writing habits, working methodically for shorter periods more frequently—at least three days each week. Boice frequently visited the offices of these sixteen professors while they were writing, observed the speed and duration of their writing sessions, administered psychological tests to measure levels of mania and depression, and kept track of their long-term productivity and general success in their fields.

The results of this study indicated that perceptions of creativity and productivity among the binge writers were false impressions, probably stimulated by the hypomanic state itself. Compared with their moderate colleagues, the binge writers produced "a much lower output of pages, one that fell well short of their projections for sufficient numbers to gain tenure. . . . " While they imagined that they were highly inspired while they were writing madly for long periods, their work was judged less creative by colleagues, they had lower rates of acceptance from publications, and they were less likely to be promoted to tenure than their "plodding" counterparts. Binge writers also experienced much higher levels of emotional disturbance and mood swings, and they were more vulnerable to writing blocks following their intense writing sessions. "Depression, not genius," Boice concludes, "was the most likely outcome of their writing habits."

Although Boice used psychological concepts and methods in his research, he did not conclude that manic-depressive tendencies *cause* binge writing and subsequent blocks. If he did, we would have to assume that an unusually high proportion of scholars are prone to pathological mood disorders. Instead, Boice argues that a widespread cultural belief in the efficacy of "creative illness" leads otherwise stable people into these bouts of intense writing, which first cause mood swings and then become self-perpetuating:

> With bingeing, depression operates in a circular fashion, perhaps first as the horse in the famous cart-and horse scenario (i.e. except when we are already depressed, depression is first the effect of bingeing and then a condition that could require more bingeing to move us past its immobility . . . unless we can be induced, probably by way of incentive and modeling, to assume the regular practice of moderations such as brief, daily sessions).

It is therefore the *idea* that binge writing is effective that needs to be removed, not some personality disorder that favors this kind of writing behavior. "In the simple, democratic view taken here," Boice concludes, "strong depression is avoidable and unnecessary in writing. Any reasonably educated person, I imagine, can write productively, creatively, without it."

While I agree with these conclusions, I want to add a slightly modified theory about the causes of binge writing and subsequent blocking at high levels of academic work.

I have heard graduate students and faculty members in fields such as literary studies refer to famous, anguished writers as models for creative productivity. Perhaps in the sciences and social sciences there are comparable models of tormented genius partly responsible for bursts of intense labor followed by exhaustion and malaise. As I noted in the previous section, the idea of the elusive Muse who appears in states of delirium and disorder is a popular theory of creativity.

Among advanced graduate students, however, habits of writing cultivated in undergraduate work are more often responsible for efforts to push a writing project to completion in long, exhausting sessions, typically late at night. These methods are more effective, sometimes even necessary, in work on undergraduate papers due in the next day or two, in the midst of many other assignments. Many writers become habituated to these conditions for writing, and to a mental and physical sense that writing emerges under pressure. When they do not feel this pressure that they associate with writing, they don't write, and perhaps even feel they *can't* write. Students who use these methods often make analogies to childbirth to describe their belief that texts take shape gradually in the mind and then—when the time is ripe and the pressure to write builds sufficiently—burst forth onto the page all at once. They expect the experience of writing, when it finally occurs, to be a mixture of pain, exhilaration, and relief.

Short papers for undergraduate courses can emerge more or less in this fashion, but whole dissertations and books cannot. Professional articles rarely do, and for most purposes the analogy to childbirth is a false, debilitating conception of the writing process. It does explain, however, why blocked writers often seem to be waiting, making elaborate preparations for the time when the project is wholly conceived, ready to be written. Undergraduate work provides very few occasions for regular, routine, sustained work on long writing projects. And prior to the dissertation phase of graduate work, writing habits form almost entirely under pressure, in response to course assignments.

I strongly suspect that habits formed in undergraduate work are partly responsible for "bingeing" and subsequent blocks at professorial levels as well. This explanation does not contradict Boice's emphasis on the romantic belief in "creative illness" as a source of energy for writing, since many undergraduates hold similar beliefs that they write best in marathon sessions under intense pressure, when deadlines loom. I simply add that this belief persists, against mounting evidence against it, because writers continue to link the activity of writing with strong physical and even biochemical sensations rooted habitually in past experience. The routine, gradual assembly of a text—without pressure, without the rush of adrenaline—feels "wrong" because writing in the past has always occurred under more stressful conditions.

COSTS AND BENEFITS

Because he closely observed the methods of a small number of junior professors, Robert Boice did not attempt to estimate the frequency of writing blocks among scholars, or to answer the question I posed in the second section of this chapter: *Do writing blocks become more or less frequent beyond graduate studies, in professorial ranks of scholarship?*

When we consider the rhetorical factors that cause and relieve difficulty for writers, we can find some of both in the positions of faculty members. Some features of these positions support the hypothesis that severe writing problems increase beyond graduate school. At professorial levels of academic disciplines, standards for writing continue to rise, writing tasks become somewhat more complex, and audiences become potentially more critical. More specifically, standards for the publication of books and articles are usually higher than those for dissertations and papers in graduate work, partly because audiences for academic publications represent broader bases of knowledge and authority in the field. Peer reviewers and editors expose authors to detailed criticism of work in progress.

Other factors can add to the pressures of writing, especially for assistant professors at research universities. At schools that maintain graduate and research programs, publication is the main criterion for tenure, and scholars who do not complete writing are rarely promoted. In these positions, furthermore, professors must find periods of time for research and writing in the midst of teaching, advising, committee work, and other responsibilities that can easily distract them from sustained attention to writing projects. Fragmented schedules offer another possible explanation for the frequency of binge writing among professors. In most cases, finding time for writing is more challenging for faculty members than it is for advanced graduate students, who often have a year or two to devote primarily to dissertation projects. The case of Sarah, noted in the previous chapter, demonstrates how faculty responsibilities can complicate the difficulties of writing a dissertation. There is little reason to suppose that it is easier to find time for other kinds of professional writing among these demands. While fortunate graduate students receive guidance from advisors and support from writing groups, professors outside the sciences are more likely to write in isolation, behind closed doors.

Pamela Richards suggests that this isolation often results from competition and distrust among colleagues. As a young tenured professor of sociology, Richards wrote an essay called "Risk," published in Howard Becker's *Writing for Social Scientists*, as a reply to Becker's advice that to get out of the doldrums she should essentially "freewrite" a quick, rough draft of a new project for which she had completed research. In the form of a long letter, Richards explained why writing freely seems very dangerous for a young faculty member who feels she must constantly look over her shoulder and watch every step, to control the impressions she is making on colleagues.

Even among friends, Richards argues, this wariness results from a pervasive, relentless effort to appear smarter than other people in your field. As a consequence, if you show a rough draft of a manuscript to colleagues for help in sorting out problems, you are vulnerable to judgments about your worth as a scholar. "Peers read your work and say 'Hell, that's not so bright. I could do better than that. She's not so hot after all.' . . . The discipline is set up in such a competitive fashion that we assuage our own insecurities by denigrating others, often publicly." Richards notes that some of this premature judgment results not from malice but from the fact that "Few people understand what working drafts are."

> They assume that first drafts are just one step removed from being sent out for review. So if you show up with a working first draft, you worry about what could happen. They could decide that it's shoddy work, poorly constructed, and really quite sloppy. Their conclusion? That you're not much of a sociologist if you pass around such crap. And what if they tell that to others?

These doubts can easily afflict scholars while they are composing drafts, even if they have no intention of showing them to colleagues. *Does this sound stupid?* they ask themselves. *Can I really call this professional sociology (or philosophy, or literary criticism)?* At this stage of a new project, even experienced, established scholars can feel that they are, in Richard's terms, "frauds," and that underlying doubt can induce blocks that make failure a self-fulfilling prophecy:

So there I am, faced with a blank page, confronting the risk of discovering that I cannot do what I set out to do, and therefore am not the person I pretend to be. I haven't yet written anything down, so no one can help me affirm my commitment and underscore my sense of who I am.

Competition, distrust, and accompanying insecurities partly explain why the actual writing methods of scholars remain largely hidden and mysterious well beyond graduate school. Young professors learn to write for publication much as they learn to teach: almost entirely through trial and error, with little direct guidance from colleagues. As a consequence, the difficult transitions that begin in the dissertation phase of graduate work often continue through many years of professional life. In an unpublished memoir called "Notes on Writing in and After Graduate School," John Forester, now a professor of city and regional planning at Cornell, recalls his bewilderment over the productivity of faculty members both at Berkeley, where he was a graduate student, and UC Santa Cruz, where he began to teach.

My professors had taught me a great deal, but not much at all about writing. . . . The Berkeley faculty's own writing varied enormously, of course, and though in the slow moments of my dissertation I sought advice, the idiosyncratic anecdotes I heard didn't seem ultimately to do much for me. How could they? One prolific sociologist wrote on different projects in different places and at different times. Another distinguished sociologist told me something about trying to write ten pages a day, but I was too stunned to ask, "ten?!?" A planning professor had fifteen projects "in the pipeline" at any given time, and out came whatever he needed to respond to outside demands as they came along. But how, I wondered, did he write his books? Still another professor ruminated one May day, "Boy, how many Bic pens I'm going to go through this summer!" If I was prepared to write or knew anything about it, I was the last one to know it.

Yet in his own fashion Forester *did* gradually find ways to complete projects for publication, as did his colleagues in their own ways. In spite of additional challenges at this stage of one's career, I suspect that writing blocks become somewhat less common in professorial ranks than in graduate programs.

One obvious reason is that almost all of the people hired for tenure-track positions have already completed dissertations, and have usually published articles as well. Even if they had great difficulty in the process, they have cleared that hurdle with some confidence that they can clear others that lie ahead. Or from a perspective more grimly Darwinian, attrition fairly or unfairly weeds out many of the graduate students most vulnerable to writing blocks, and tenure decisions weed out more at the next level. To varying degrees, professors have already demonstrated, to themselves and to peers, that they can write productively, and in the entire system of higher education productivity in writing is a strong selection factor, as Northrup Frye complained even in 1958, in his address "Humanities in a New World":

> Above all, the ideal of productivity, the vision of the unobstructed assembly line, has taken over the university as it has everything else. The professor today is less a learned man than a "productive scholar." He is trained in graduate school to become productive by an ingenious but simple device. . . . Our graduate student today must finish a thesis, a document which is, practically by definition, something that nobody particularly wants either to write or to read. This teaches him that it is more important to produce than to perfect, and that it is less anti-social to contribute to knowledge than to possess it.

But there are more positive factors that help scholars to overcome the difficulties they experienced while writing dissertations. Academic publications, for example, are not liminal texts. They have identifiable forms, functions, and audiences within professional communities, beyond the idiosyncratic expectations of individual readers. It is therefore somewhat easier for scholars to determine what they are writing, who they are as authors, and what readers are likely to expect. Guidelines for submission, editorial guidance, and peer reviews help to answer these questions as well.

In most cases, furthermore, professional writing emerges gradually and in a variety of forms from a larger frame of reference in which particular questions become significant. A scholar's research and its relations to other research provide a repository of potential writing projects "in the pipeline" at various stages, often beginning with talks or papers at professional conferences. At conferences, scholars also receive direct affirmation and criticism that helps them to figure out where their work stands. Articles frequently evolve from these presentations. Books frequently evolve from the topics of articles. Publications can therefore become the extensions of professional conversations, and seem less hypothetical as forms of communication. Through this organic process, scholarly writing rarely begins with the question *What should I write about?*

Within this process, time pressure can be an advantage over the great expanse of time many graduate students must figure out how to use productively. John Forester links the genesis of most of the articles he published to unavoidable deadlines for conference papers:

> If I had to present a paper in Baltimore at a conference of the American Planning Association, I knew that I had to have a paper in hand (indeed, twenty copies) by the day I'd have to leave home. Deadlines concentrate the mind and move the typewriter keys. Most of what I've written, and certainly the best of it, has been written originally for conference obligations that I'd taken on months ahead of time. For months I'd ruminate, collect notes on the side, make false starts, and have the pressure slowly build, until finally I produced a draft, honoring earlier outlines or not, that I could show others. Those drafts I usually submitted *quickly* to journals for possible publication.
>
> I learned a fundamental rule: never, never, never to sit on a draft, to withhold a decent draft from the review of the referees of appropriate journals.

Forester is certainly not alone in his tendency to write most productively under the pressure of tight deadlines. I know faculty members who use their time for writing *least* productively when they have the most to spend: during sabbatical leaves devoted to writing books. Like dissertation writers, they can become lost in the enormity of the task. In another study, described in his essay "Psychotherapies for Writing Blocks," Robert Boice found evidence that the necessity of producing certain amounts of writing each day increases the productivity and quality of academic writing. When he told one group of scholars that they had to produce writing five days each week and left another group to write spontaneously, whenever they felt inclined to write, the first, "contingency" group was far more productive. Having generated an average of 0.4 page per day before the controls were imposed, they wrote 3.2 pages per day during the control period and reported a significant increase in creative ideas as well. The writers left to their own inclinations became only slightly more productive, moving from 0.3 to 0.9 page per day without significant rise in creativity. Boice concludes that behavioral modifications, toward established schedules and quotas, can improve both the quality and quantity of a writer's output. Lots of time and freedom to write when inspiration moves us can have the opposite results.

In this respect, the phrase "in the pipeline" puts writing in its appropriate place, as an assembly line for writing projects in the midst of other interests and commitments. The phrase also suggests the movement of these projects through manageable stages of completion, so that writers are working on something in particular at a certain stage in its development. They are less likely to become wholly immersed, then, in single tasks that seem impossibly broad and complex.

Taken together, all of these factors suggest that you are most likely to complete writing projects successfully when you establish regular periods of time wholly devoted to writing at regular intervals, with moderate but clear expectations for the amount of work you will complete. Because most of us cannot sustain this work for more than three or four hours a day, other responsibilities are not detrimental to the completion of writing projects unless they continually fragment time for sustained writing or create distraction. Open stretches of time without deadlines can even induce writing blocks if you do not deliberately structure the use of this time, with regular, modest expectations.

What Can You Do?

A Writer is someone for whom writing is more difficult than it is for other people.

THOMAS MANN

THE NORMALITY OF WRITING BLOCKS

Throughout this book I have tried to demystify writing blocks by examining the methods, conceptions, and circumstances through which these difficulties arise in academic writing. These factors are complex, but mystification often occurs when we oversimplify matters of real complexity. It would be easier to understand and cure "writer's block," perhaps, if this malady resulted from a specific kind of psychological disorder that certain kinds of people experience. The rest of us could then safely assume that we were immune to this type of "mental block" that bore little relation to normal writing difficulties.

The writers who encounter a block often accept this simplistic, popular explanation precisely because their problems arise from ordinary writing projects and activities. The fact that less capable and motivated students completed the same assignments without difficulty contributed to Carmen's feeling that there was something mysteriously wrong with her. Graduate students and professors who fail to complete writing projects know other scholars who produce the same kinds of papers, articles, dissertations, or books under similar circumstances. It is difficult to avoid thinking *It's just me.* Yet this idea further confuses individuals who have become immobilized in the writing process, and offers no real solution. If they come to believe that the causes of their writing problems lie in their personalities, they are less likely to examine the real contexts in which their struggles occur.

If we look at these contexts, we can see that they are more or less normal, and so are the writers. In fact it is difficult to distinguish the typical blocked writer from the most common notion of a good, successful writer and scholar. Blocked writers are usually both capable and highly motivated. Their strong intellectual interests in the subjects they write about are informed by extensive reading and knowledge. As a rule blocked writers, like other good writers, have high standards for their work and are rarely satisfied with their first thoughts. As a consequence, they tend to revise plans and drafts extensively as they move through the process, and if doubts or better approaches occur to them, they stop to alter the text rather than settling for the version they have already produced. No one in higher education would consider deep intellectual interests, high standards for finished work, and extensive revision to be weak, abnormal traits for scholarly writers. Most writing teachers encourage these attitudes and practices as foundations for good writing.

In turn, most of the symptoms of writing blocks occur quite commonly in academic writing. If we could observe the most thoughtful, successful students and scholars at work on a writing project, at a given moment we might find them stuck in a difficult passage, dissatisfied, and frustrated with the task. We might find that progress has been delayed for hours, days, or weeks. At that moment they might be moving back through loops of rereading, rethinking, and revision, without knowing for certain where this movement will take them. Or we might find them at the library, gathering or reading further reference material to clarify their approaches and gain momentum for moving ahead. At those moments it would be impossible to distinguish blocked writers from those who were making gradual progress in an unavoidably loopy fashion. Good writers who can avoid these loops, delays, and frustrations are extremely rare.

Even the most direct, circumstantial causes of writing blocks are fairly common features of academic contexts for writing. From the first year of undergraduate work through professorial ranks, writing usually occurs under the pressure of deadlines and competing demands for the writer's attention. All undergraduates in fields that require extensive writing must complete papers under tight schedules and must adapt to increasingly challenging, complex assignments. The great majority of graduate students must contend with the ambiguities of the dissertation phase and with the challenges of producing a book-length work of scholarship for the first time. A large proportion of these graduate students must complete dissertations without focused attention and constructive guidance from advisors. Dysfunctional, obstructive graduate committees are common hazards of graduate work. The intense pressure to publish in the midst of teaching and other responsibilities is a standard condition of life for scholars, especially in tenure track positions as assistant professors. And in these positions high standards for finished work in competitive fields are inescapable realities, not the neuroses of "perfectionists."

In short, the conditions from which writing blocks arise are fairly ordinary, sometimes pervasive features of academic life. Because we write in the midst of our lives, in our bodies, in the world, there is no reason to suppose that writing should be any less complex than the other things we do. Nor is it surprising that people should run into many kinds of difficulty while they are engaged in this complicated endeavor. In some respects writing poses special difficulties because, as I noted in Chapter 2, while we are engaged in this activity its outcome—communication with readers—remains imaginary. While we are writing, therefore, it is very easy for us to become distracted from what we are actually doing by anticipation of the outcome.

It is possible that the mystification of writing blocks represents an effort to deny these normal difficulties, to keep them at bay, or to maintain the illusion that the truly Good Writers we should all emulate just sit down and write beautifully without effort. In his preface to *Writing Without Teachers*, Peter Elbow both acknowledged this illusion and shattered it, to the great relief of many struggling writers:

> The authority I call upon in writing a book about writing is my own long-standing difficulty in writing. It has always seemed to me as though people who wrote without turmoil and torture were in a completely different universe. And yet advice about writing always seemed to come from them and therefore to bear no relation to those of us who struggled and usually failed to write. But in the last few years I have struggled more successfully to get things written and make them work for at least some readers, and in watching myself do this I have developed the conviction that I can give advice that speaks more directly to the experience of having a hard time writing, I have also reached the conviction that if you have special difficulty in writing, you are not necessarily further from writing well than someone who writes more easily.

When they are discussing their problems, blocked writers often describe this sense of proximity to effective, productive writing. "I feel like the barrier between not writing and writing is tissue thin," one student said. "I can see through it to the other side and picture myself there, writing away. I can imagine how that would be. I just can't seem to break through and get there."

The similarities between blocks and ordinary writing difficulties explain why people who were getting nowhere with a project for several months can suddenly become productive writers, indistinguishable from others. When the misconceptions, inappropriate methods, or rhetorical conditions that immobilize writers are removed, blocks often vanish without a trace. Sometimes these changes seem minor: a slight shift in one's conception of the task; a change of method and behavior at a certain moment in the process that breaks the circle; or the clarification of an advisor's expectations. Like the small motion of turning a key, however, these minor changes can transform a dead end into an open corridor. Moving beyond this barrier, the writer is not a substantially different person, with an altered personality. Differences in her mood or in conditions of her life simply result from movement itself as opposed to stasis: from the experience and consequences of finally getting things written.

THE REALITY OF A WRITING BLOCK

If writing blocks emerge from the ordinary practices and difficulties of good writers engaged in complex tasks, how can you tell whether you are really blocked or not?

I can answer that question most simply with another question: *Are you making progress with writing projects or are you getting nowhere?*

I recognize, however, that at particular moments this second question can be difficult to answer. When you have just decided that a draft you have started is going in the wrong direction and needs extensive revision, this decision will not feel like progress unless you have confidence that you can produce a better version. If you feel that you need to stop writing to clarify your position through further reading, that interruption might or might not eventually carry your writing forward. At these moments, productive writers sometimes feel they are getting nowhere and blocked writers sometimes feel that starting over or pausing to read is an "essential delay."

But where have these decisions at these moments taken you in the long run? If you are encountering a writing block, you will find that they carry you habitually through the same cycles of activity, for the same reasons, back to the same place in the writing process. And at that place—as you begin to compose a new introduction, perhaps, or revise a literature review—you will feel once again that you can't go on until you do something else: take a break, do further reading, make additional notes or outlines, reorganize your workspace. . . . When he stepped back to observe the way these moments comprise patterns, Carl noticed that when he had written two or three pages of a draft the pen actually fell from his hand, as though it were telling him he must stop. Physically, the problem was simply "writer's cramp," caused by the tension in his hand and forearm while he wrote. The real writing problem, however, was that he did not let his arm rest and return to the draft, or compose on a keyboard instead. Without pausing to consider this stimulus/response pattern, he turned away from the draft when the pen dropped, and when he eventually returned to the task he invariably viewed the old draft as a false start.

Before Carl recognized this pattern, he knew that something was wrong. Although he felt at specific moments that he must stop composing a draft in order to continue, in a larger sense he knew he wasn't getting anywhere.

In somewhat different terms, you can tell whether a writing block is real to the extent that writing remains *unrealized* in at least one of the two ways in which writing is real.

1. *Writing is a real psychophysical activity*: something we are either doing or not doing at a given time. Hemingway liked to write while standing, but for most of us writing occurs when we are sitting somewhere, at a desk or table perhaps, with paper and pen or with a keyboard. Our hands move. Thought and language converge in this motion. Words form in sequence. A sentence unfolds. Another sentence follows. This, quite simply, is the activity of writing, and it occurs not just in our minds but when we are actually, physically there—not somewhere else or nowhere at all.

For students and scholars, especially, other kinds of related activity usually surround writing. When the wires of language and thought disconnect and I lose that current that keeps me moving, I usually go for a short walk. This frequently happens when the computer screen becomes overbearing or I get restless from sitting. While I'm walking, I let myself think in sentences and listen to the way they sound, say them over to myself, and alter them until I've restored the connection and can return to writing with some momentum. Or I might pause to read something, to locate a quotation or clarify a point of confusion. These and other activities are directly related to writing and occur within the writing process.

They contribute to forward movement, however, only if they lead us directly back to the text we were producing and are thus dedicated to its continuation or revision. Going for a walk and thinking about writing is not productive unless I return immediately to the text and resume the activity of putting words on paper. If I stop to talk to someone or for other reasons do not return to my work, I lose the thoughts and sentences that would have carried me forward. The same is true of reading. If I become absorbed in reading for its own sake, as an activity separate from writing, the text I am reading will carry me away from my own work, until I can't remember why I stopped to read, what I was looking for, or the direction my own text was taking. As a scholar I might imagine that while reading I am still "writing" in a broader sense, but I am not.

2. *The text you produce through this activity is also real.* The words and sentences that materialize on the page are no longer just your thoughts, your intentions to say something. If you go off for hours, weeks, or even years and return these sentences will still be there unchanged, even if *you* have changed and now perceive them differently. When language and thought have taken this form of an object, they can also become a form of communication with others if you choose to release your work to readers. And this textual object can, in a sense, live without you. Texts commonly outlive their authors. When you are actually writing, therefore, you produce a real object: something that can be seen and heard.

It might seem obvious that this second realization of writing depends upon the first. In other words, you can't gain the benefits of the product (as the story of "The Little Red Hen" reminds us) without going through the process. You can't expect to end up with a real text, even in a rough draft, without actually investing the time and attention required to produce it, sentence by sentence, page by page.

But writers are often strangely oblivious to this simple relation between actually putting words on paper and actually having things written. Their behavior suggests that finished writing might emerge, almost effortlessly, through detailed preparations and intentions. Perhaps this is why struggling writers are fond of analogies to gestation and childbirth, as I observed in the previous chapter. They feel that the finished work is growing and developing inside them, through the nourishment of reading, thinking, notes, and plans. When this conception and gestation of the work is complete, the project will be virtually finished. A brief, intense period of real labor will occur and the book, dissertation, or essay will appear essentially intact, needing only to be cleaned up before it is ready to be shown to the world. Perhaps this misconception (if you will excuse the pun) also explains why writers often spend so much time organizing the surroundings in which they expect this miraculous event to occur.

Academic writers might be especially vulnerable to this idea, simply because works of scholarship usually require extensive reading, notes, data analysis, and other preparations for writing. It is easy for us to convince ourselves that just a bit more reading and planning will make the actual task of producing the text more efficient. But novelists and poets have also contributed to the belief that writing emerges from the fully ripened imagination or inspiration. "As for my next book," Virginia Woolf noted in her diary in 1928, "I am going to hold myself from writing till I have it impending in me: grown heavy in my mind like a ripe pear; pendant, gravid, asking to be cut or it will fall."

As some of the examples in this book demonstrate, overpreparation can make the actual task of writing more frustrating, less efficient, or even impossible. In their efforts to assemble fully developed plans for writing from an unassailable position of authority and understanding, blocked writers have often created expectations for themselves that they can never meet. Attempts to implement these plans therefore suggest that the time for real writing is not yet ripe. Perhaps further reading, further notes and thoughts, will bring the product of their preparations about.

In fact, *preparation for writing never brings writing about.* Sustained passages of text result only from sustained periods of composing text. For this reason writing is not like conceiving and giving birth to a child. It is more like building something, such as a piece of furniture: the physical assembly, from raw materials, of contiguous parts into a whole. Some people prefer to fashion and assemble these parts from detailed designs; others prefer to let the form emerge from the process of assembly itself. If it is real, however, the product must result from the assembly, not just from the design.

If you question whether you are really a blocked writer, therefore, you simply need to ask yourself whether real writing, in both of these senses and over time, has actually occurred.

WHAT YOU CAN DO

If you feel immobilized in the writing process, this book should have provided you with the conceptual and diagnostic tools to identify the causes of the problem. For this purpose, the most fundamental tools are the questions I posed in the first chapter:

What kind of writing are you trying to do?

How do you approach this task?

At what point, exactly, does progress end?

What do you do up to that point?

When you reach it, what do you do next, and why?

Understanding of the writing process and the unavoidable loopiness of movement through it should help you locate that place where progress comes to a halt. Examples of blocked writers should help you identify the misconceptions, patterns of behavior, and circumstances that surround this obstacle. As I've noted, the great majority of writing blocks are transitional. They occur, in other words, when writers have moved into unfamiliar contexts for writing, with different forms, audiences, and standards for finished work. Blocks tend to occur when writers try to use old methods in these new contexts, or when the strategies they develop are "maladaptive." If this is the case, the questions I listed above can help you figure out how your writing strategies need to change.

In my experience, all struggling writers can answer these questions, and in some cases I don't even need to ask them. These writers have already assembled a clear understanding of the problem and know what they need to do differently. They simply need to explain this understanding to someone who will listen and tell them whether it makes sense, often because the notion that a block is a mysterious neurosis undermines their confidence that the problem can be solved so methodically. In many cases this articulation and confirmation of the problem provides enough incentive for writers to change their strategies, and the writing block simply vanishes.

I'm aware that a book cannot entirely replace this consultation, in which understandings emerge from conversation about specific projects and situations. I know that I can't reliably predict what you are doing and need to be doing as individual writers.

To give you confidence in your own ability to solve these problems, however, I should mention that understandings and solutions result largely from what these individual writers tell me, not from what I tell them. For this reason you should be able to use this book to explain the nature of your writing difficulties to yourself, and find solutions.

I wish I could recommend with greater confidence that you should find assistance with these writing difficulties on your own campus. Some universities have begun to offer workshops on writing for graduate students, and if you are writing a dissertation you can contact your graduate school office to find out if such workshops are available. If they are not, you might encourage your school to offer them, because the need is much greater than university administrators imagine. A friend at a large university recently told me that when they offered the first workshop on dissertation writing they expected ten or twenty graduate students to attend. The workshop drew two hundred.

Most universities do have writing centers, and although these services are primarily for undergraduates who need to write better papers, experienced staff members can often provide useful advice for capable writers entangled in the process of writing. Outside these centers, good writing teachers might be able to suggest alternative strategies, even if they have not worked extensively with writing blocks.

Before you look for advice, however, you should develop at least a tentative understanding of the problem with which you can listen to this advice critically. People who are willing to listen and respond thoughtfully to your difficulties are rarer than those who will offer suggestions based on their own misunderstanding of writing blocks. I have known desperate writers who tried to follow every recommendation made by well-meaning friends and teachers, and became increasingly confused in the process.

Here are some further suggestions for using the concepts in this book to resolve your own writing problems:

• *When you consider the questions listed above, write down your answers.* Then read over what you have written, think about what you have said, and write a set of recommendations for changes you need to make in your writing strategies. What I've said before about the difference between reading and writing applies here as well. Just reading this book isn't going to transform you into a productive writer, even it helps you to understand why you aren't one, any more than reading will get your writing projects done. You won't begin to change in any useful way until you apply this understanding to your own work, in practice. Toward this end, explaining to yourself what is wrong and what you need to do is a good start.

• *Put this understanding into practice.* If you can tell yourself what you think is wrong and what you need to do, the next step is to make the changes you recommend. You can think of this as experimental research. If the strategies you develop don't work, or if you have trouble following your own advice, don't fall back into the old approach as a default mode, simply because it is the familiar (and in some ways comfortable) way of doing things. If it hasn't worked in the past it isn't going to work now. Instead, go back to the drawing board. Try to explain to yourself in writing what went wrong and why, and what you should do next, as you would in research notes or a lab notebook. Then try that strategy.

• *Along similar lines, deliberately inhibit yourself from doing things you suspect to be at the heart of the problem, even if they seem, at the moment, to be necessary.* If a familiar way of writing doesn't work, you obviously need to do something different at that moment, even if it seems odd or uncomfortable. If you habitually interrupt your writing because you feel compelled to read something, and if you suspect that this habit undermines your work, you will not solve the problem until you recognize that this is a choice and deliberately choose *not* to interrupt your work, even if this decision feels "wrong" at the moment. If you are in the habit of writing at times or places that are unproductive, find times or places that work better.

• *To the extent that you can, compartmentalize your writing projects and your writing difficulties.* Struggling writers tend to keep working harder and thinking more about their writing in the effort to surmount their problems. If you are already spending enormous amounts of time on this work without much to show for it, more time, effort, and thought will not make you more productive. And while the pressures and frustrations of writing are difficult to compartmentalize, they tend to interfere with pleasure and effectiveness in other dimensions of our lives. Most of that interference is unnecessary. As you begin to explore ways of writing more productively, try to keep this work confined to periods of no more than four hours. When this time is over and you turn your attention to something or someone else, try to forget your writing and do those other things wholeheartedly.

• *If you don't have a clear sense for the kind of writing you are trying to produce, find models for this project and look at them carefully.* Highly motivated writers tend to feel that their work should be completely original, and perhaps this is why they also tend to ignore useful models. I've noted that graduates students often feel that they must reinvent the genre of the dissertation in their fields, and rarely look at dissertations completed for their advisors. Examples of papers written for specific courses are not so readily available, but teachers will sometimes recommend published essays that show you the kinds of writing they are looking for. Models for articles and books in a discipline are easy to locate. When you find examples as close as possible to your own work, pay attention to the scope of the topic, the way the author set forth the central problem or position, and the way the text moves from beginning to end—its organization. Note the tone and style. Don't be reluctant to emulate features you like, or to depart from ones you dislike. We learn to use language almost entirely through imitation and avoidance.

• *If you are working on a complex project, try to avoid isolation with the task.* If you are working on an undergraduate research paper, for example, talk with other students about what you and they are doing, exchange drafts of work in progress, or talk to someone in the writing center, especially if you are having trouble. If you are working on a graduate dissertation, make the effort to form a writing group to discuss projects, and propose talks on the topic at professional conferences. If you are working on a book or a research article, find colleagues who share your interests and talk about your project, or exchange material with someone who is also writing.

• *Finally, if you turn to someone for advice about difficulties in completing writing projects, don't feel that you should announce "I have writer's block!"* You might feel uncomfortable about this label (as though you were announcing "I'm neurotic!"), and for related reasons the label isn't likely to be useful. I've found the term "block" useful to describe real obstacles to movement through the writing process, but if you describe your difficulties in this way, the advice you get will be conditioned by the other person's understanding or misunderstanding of the term. And as I've pointed out, the misconceptions prevail. Instead, describe as clearly as you can the specific kind of problem you are having: e.g., "I just can't seem to get past the introduction," or "The more I read about the subject, the less I know what I want to say." If you have ideas about possible solutions, explain what they are.

I stress your active, critical role in these consultations because if you are encountering a writing block, you are the only person who can move beyond it. To a great extent I can describe what these obstacles are, where and why they are most likely to occur, and how other writers have gotten past them. Clearer understanding should loosen the ideas and practices that immobilize you, and should stimulate a sense of release from their grip. But I can't actually remove this obstacle from your path, and neither can anyone else. All of the blocked writers I have known who began to write productively have actually changed what they were previously doing, in minor ways or in major ways, suddenly or very slowly. Figuring out what changes you should make is therefore half of the challenge. Actually making those changes is the other half.

A Note to Teachers and Advisors

Advice I've offered to writers in this book should also provide guidance for teachers, advisors, and friends of struggling writers. The questions I told blocked writers to ask themselves, for example, are ones that teachers or advisors can ask students who seem mired in writing projects.

- What kind of writing are you trying to do?
- How do you approach this task?
- At what point, exactly, does progress end?
- What do you do up to that point?
- When you reach it, what do you do next, and why?

Selecting advice that seems most useful in a particular case, you can also offer writers most of the suggestions I listed at the end of the last chapter.

I'll briefly make some other guidance more explicit, considering the different roles of teachers and advisors.

WHAT TEACHERS CAN DO

For reasons I've explained, writing blocks can be difficult to distinguish from other kinds of difficulties, delays, and failures among student writers. In most undergraduate courses we know very little about the ways in which individual students complete the papers we assign, or about the reasons for which some of them fail to complete assignments. If you ask them directly why their papers are missing or consistently late, struggling writers will not necessarily tell you they are struggling with writing itself, or that they are "blocked." Following profuse apologies, they might say they are really busy this semester, that they didn't have as much time for the paper as they needed, that they had trouble finding some of the references, or that they started the project too late. They will probably tell you that the paper, or papers, will be finished on Monday.

And these are not necessarily deceptions. When transitional blocks suddenly occur, writers don't immediately understand what is wrong, and they tend to view their difficulty as a personal problem or weakness, not as a legitimate excuse or as something teachers can help to resolve. They might genuinely believe, for good reasons, that they have too much work and too many distractions, or that they should have started the project earlier. They probably believe, as well, that they will meet the new deadline they announce to you and set for themselves, though blocked writers rarely do.

Students also fail to complete papers or turn them in late for a variety of reasons, and among undergraduates writing blocks are not the most common causes. Procrastination, competing priorities, unexpected crises, and general malaise are more often responsible for late and missing work. If writers themselves have trouble distinguishing these causes from obstacles in the writing process, you will have even more difficulty doing so.

Then why should you worry about these problems?

Entanglements in the writing process are real writing problems, not just idiosyncratic personal disorders, and if you are a writing teacher specific students will both need and deserve your help with these problems. If you are not a writing teacher, but assign writing in your courses, very capable students who have learned a great deal might perform poorly, or even fail your course, for reasons that have little to do with their ability, effort, knowledge, interest, and other criteria you value in grading. Good teachers want to know who these students are, to help them directly, or to help them find help.

This book does offer some clues for identifying blocked writers, and I'll offer a couple of further suggestions specifically for teachers. I'm thinking especially of undergraduates here, but most of these observations also apply to graduate students who are writing in courses:

• Individuals most vulnerable to writing blocks will usually be among the most capable, motivated, and thoughtful students in your class. They might be either shy or vocal in the classroom. If they participate, they will ask complex questions and make interesting observations that you will expect to form the basis of excellent papers. Shy students might express these views in conferences or let you know in other ways that they are thinking deeply about the course material. Both types will tend to propose very ambitious paper topics. When the papers do not appear, or if these students turn in rough notes with the promise of finished work to come, you will find this gap between their promise and their performance rather mysterious. The same kind of mystery will arise if they turn in exceptionally good work and then fail to complete the next assignment. That sense of mystery suggests an obstacle in the writing process.

• Blocks tend to arise in the fields and courses students care the most about—typically in their major concentrations and for teachers the students want most to impress. In these circumstances, standards for quality and complexity are most likely to rise beyond the writer's performance in the moment, creating continual dissatisfaction with work in progress.

• Especially if you are teaching a writing course, you can identify potential blocks and other problems by asking students, fairly early in the term, to write informally about the methods they use for writing, and any difficulties they encounter in the process. These papers provide useful material for discussions and conferences, and they serve as later points of reference if specific students run into trouble.

• More generally, make actual methods of writing the subject of a writing course, or the subject of specific class sessions in other courses that assign a lot of writing. This attention will help to depersonalize difficulties in the writing process, reduce the isolation of struggling writers, and prevent some kinds of writing blocks.

• When you have identified students who are having trouble completing papers, schedule individual conferences to discuss the problem, as soon as possible. First ask these students to describe the problem in their own terms. If they indicate general stress, depression, family crises, or other personal problems, you might want to recommend psychological counseling. If they focus on problems with their writing projects, even in terms of surrounding distractions and pressures, use the questions I've listed above to identify when and where the obstacle occurs, and suggest some alternative methods.

• For assignments in your classes, the standards blocked writers are trying to meet are the ones they imagine that you hold, or ones they impose on themselves for the purpose of impressing you. In either case, you are implicated in their difficulties. If you find that writers are trying to do something nearly impossible, or well beyond your expectations, you need to help them revise their expectations to a level at which writing is easier. The direction of this help might run against your own habitual tendency to push students to higher levels of performance. But blocked writers are already pushing themselves *beyond* their optimal levels of performance. Narrower focus and lower standards will *improve* their writing.

• While I've used the term *writing block* to demystify a category of writing difficulties, I tend to avoid using this term in my conversations with students. Popular associations of "writer's block" with psychological disorder are so strong that the label undermines attempts to understand why specific writers are having trouble. While asking the questions listed above, you can avoid these associations by referring, for example, to "obstacles in the writing process."

• Grades and deadlines are complicated issues for blocked writers, and for their teachers. When generous teachers learn that capable students are struggling with complex projects, their first impulse is to extend the deadline. More time, however, will rarely solve the problem if the writer doesn't understand what is wrong. Instead, standards for performance and performance anxieties continue to rise, in the writer's effort to justify the extra time and compensate for previous failures. Blocked writers will think, "Now the paper has to be *really* good." In these situations I try to set the issues of deadlines and grades aside as much as possible, to clear a space in which we can focus on the writing problem itself, as a goal for instruction. In types of courses where this is impossible, you might as well stick with the regular schedule and grading criteria, and offer as much help as you can within that course structure. When I start to postpone deadlines and forgive missing papers, the writer's difficulties usually worsen, along with the problem of grading at the end of the term.

• If you find that you can't understand or help to resolve a student's difficulties, contact the writing center or writing program office on your campus to identify writing teachers or tutors who have some experience working with blocked writers.

WHAT ADVISORS CAN DO

I'll briefly offer advice to undergraduate advisors and then focus on the somewhat different roles of advisors who serve on graduate committees.

The roles of undergraduate advisors vary radically both within and among campuses. Some advisors are little more than rubber stamps for a student's course selection during registration. Others serve as real mentors for advisees: someone a student can always turn to for help with academic decisions, academic difficulties, and even personal problems. Between these extremes, of course, advisors pay varying amounts of attention to a student's academic progress, grades, and career goals.

If you are monitoring the grades and general progress of advisees, there are specific signs that might indicate writing blocks and related difficulties. When students fail courses that require extensive writing, regularly drop these courses in the middle of the term, or take grades of "incomplete," this often means that they are not finishing writing assignments. Keeping in mind the possibility that they are running into obstacles in the writing process, you should ask them to explain these patterns in their record. If their responses suggest that they get derailed in the process of writing, follow the relevant advice I offered to teachers above.

If you serve as a mentor for advisees, you might be in a better position to help them than their teachers are. You do not represent the specific standards they are trying to meet. You do not have to grade their work at the end of the term. And you can more easily talk with them about their academic work in general, including patterns of difficulty visible only when we step outside the structure of a particular course.

Some undergraduates also have advisors for honors theses or senior projects, which can induce transitional writing blocks for essentially the same reasons that dissertations do. These projects are typically longer and more complex than anything the student has completed in the past. The period for completion is also longer and less structured. Procedures used for writing short papers will not necessarily work for a research-based honors thesis, and inexperienced writers tend to overestimate the breadth of an appropriate topic. Without good supervision, they can become mired in impossibly broad, murky projects that consume enormous amounts of time.

With these hazards in mind, the Department of Government at Cornell developed a Junior Honors Seminar in which faculty members teach prospective honors students how to design focused research projects in political studies. Even with such a course behind them, however, seniors who are working on honors theses need close supervision from advisors, especially in the early stages of their research. Advisors should meet with them regularly to get the research in focus, monitor progress, resolve conceptual problems, and discuss early drafts.

For reasons I've explained in Chapters 6 and 7, graduate programs should be vitally concerned about long delays and failures of students to complete dissertations. The economic and intellectual costs of these problems are extremely high, partly because struggling writers in the dissertation phase are often the most promising young scholars in their disciplines.

In a surprisingly large proportion of graduate programs, however, the dissertation is viewed simply as a test of the individual student's ability to complete a research project, not as a complex type of writing students must learn to produce, through guidance and instruction. In fact, the students who fail to complete dissertations are not, as a rule, the weakest scholars;

they are the ones who undertake the most complex projects with the least constructive support from advisors and departments.

Some departments have established systems that help to structure and supervise dissertation work at regular intervals. Required committee meetings to discuss dissertation proposals, departmental colloquia to present work in progress, workshops for dissertation writers, and the organization of writing groups can all make an otherwise lonely process a central, collective feature of graduate education. Some directors of graduate studies monitor the progress of all students in the department and communicate with advisors when specific students fall behind schedule. If your own department simply allows dissertation writers to head off into the wilderness alone, I strongly recommend that you propose and help to organize systems for making the progress of dissertation writers a departmental responsibility.

With or without these systems, graduate advisors hold the most direct responsibility for supporting work on the dissertation. Even more than teachers in undergraduate courses, graduate advisors are unavoidably implicated in the writing process. If you occupy this role, you are the primary audience for this work and the final judge of its quality. Dissertation writers are trying to meet your expectations and standards. Benign neglect—the norm in many departments—is a denial of this implication: a way of dodging real responsibility, leaving the success or failure of individual students to chance. The fact that writing blocks are much less common in the sciences than in the humanities results to a great extent from the collaborative support young scholars in the sciences receive throughout the research and writing process.

If you advise graduate students who are already in trouble with writing projects, the questions, suggestions, and examples in the body of this book should provide guidelines for helping these students. Because the majority of the writing blocks in the dissertation phase result from isolation, neglect, or misunderstandings with advisors, however, the specific advice I offer below is preventive:

- Before graduate students get very far into their research, you need to make certain that they have developed a focused research question and viable methods for pursuing this line of inquiry. The student and *all* members of the dissertation committee should reach agreement about this topic and approach, and they should remain in communication about necessary changes. Do not be reluctant to tell students directly that they need to narrow the scope of projects that seem too ambitious. Remind them that they can pursue other dimensions of this research in later books and articles.

- Do not wait for graduate students to contact you about their progress and difficulties. Many students (most in some departments) feel that the need for help is a sign of weakness, and that they should contact you only when they have made significant progress. If you do not hear from them for several months, the assumption that they do not need your help is usually false. Regularly scheduled meetings to discuss their progress help to resolve all of these issues. If the student is conducting research or writing in another state or country, regular e-mail exchanges, phone conversations, or correspondence can serve similar purposes.

- Stay in contact with other members of the graduate committee, to make sure that you have similar conceptions of the project and are not offering contradictory advice.

- Keep notes and files on the student's work and briefly review this material before meetings, to make sure that you remember the focus of the research, the stage of its development, and the central issues you need to discuss. I find that this practice saves time and allows me to offer more constructive advice. It also assures writers that someone really understands what they are doing and is paying attention to their work.

- For similar reasons, avoid making random, offhand suggestions just to make yourself feel that you are doing your job. I know of dissertation projects that were delayed for months due to remarks an advisor tossed out without thinking, because he didn't remember what the writer was actually doing. In most cases these comments suggest other kinds of literature, other theories and approaches, other directions that greatly complicate the task at hand.

- If possible, refer the student to examples of the kind of text you want him or her to produce: other dissertations, perhaps, or highly focused books in the field.

- When you read early drafts or proposals, do not line edit this writing. Address your comments to the concepts, methods, and direction of the work. If you need to tell students that their approach is flawed, be sure to suggest alternative concepts and strategies that can move the project forward. If there are glaring rhetorical and stylistic problems you must point out, confine these observations to a sample paragraph or a couple of examples. Otherwise, stylistic and editorial revision should occur after a full draft of the text is complete.

References

Alexander, F. Matthias. *The Use of the Self.* New York: Dutton, 1932.

Barthes, Roland. *Image-Music-Text.* New York: Hill and Wang, 1977.

Becker, Howard. *Writing for Social Scientists: How to Start and Finish Your Thesis, Book, or Article.* Chicago: University of Chicago Press, 1986.

Bell, Marvin. "Three Propositions: Hooey, Dewey, and Loony." In *Writers on Writing.* Ed. Robert Pack and Jay Parini. Hanover, N.H.: Middlebury College Press, 1991, pp. 1–14.

Bloom, Lynn Z. "Anxious Writers in Context: Graduate School and Beyond." In *When a Writer Can't Write.* Ed. Mike Rose. New York: Guilford Press, 1985, pp. 119–133.

Boice, Robert. "Psychotherapies for Writing Blocks." In *When a Writer Can't Write.* Ed. Mike Rose. New York: Guilford Press, 1985, pp. 182–218.

———. *How Writers Journey to Comfort and Fluency: A Psychological Adventure.* Westport: Praeger, 1994.

———. "Which Is More Productive, Writing in Binge Patterns of Creative Illness or in Moderation?" *Written Communication,* October 1997, pp. 435–459.

Cayton, Mary Kupiec. "What Happens When Things Go Wrong: Women and Writing Blocks." *Journal of Advanced Composition* 10: 321–338, 1990.

Didion, Joan. Interview. In *Women Writers at Work: The Paris Review Interviews.* Ed. George Plimpton. New York: Viking, 1989, pp. 319–336.

Dillard, Annie. *The Writing Life.* New York: Harper and Row, 1989.

Elbow, Peter. *Writing Without Teachers.* London: Oxford University Press, 1973.

———. "An Interview with Peter Elbow: 'Going in Two Directions at Once.' " *Writing on the Edge* 4.1: 9–30, 1992.

Emig, Janet. *The Composing Process of Twelfth Graders.* Urbana, Ill.: NCTE, 1971.

Flower, Linda S., and John Hayes. "The Dynamics of Composing: Making Plans and Juggling Constraints." In *Cognitive Processes in Writing.* Ed. L. W. Gregg and E. R. Steinberg. Hillsdale, N.J.: Lawrence Erlbaum Associates, 1980, pp. 31–50.

Forester, John. "Notes on Writing In and After Graduate School." Unpublished manuscript, 1984.

Friedman, Bonnie. *Writing Past Dark: Envy, Fear, Distraction, and Other Dilemmas in the Writer's Life.* New York: Harper, 1993.

143

Frye, Northrop. "Humanities in a New World." In *Writers on Writing: An Anthology*. Ed. Robert Neale. Auckland: Oxford University Press, 1992.

Geertz, Clifford. "Deep Play: Notes on the Balinese Cockfight." In *Interpretive Social Science*. Eds. Paul Rabinow and William Sullivan. Berkeley: University of California Press, 1979.

———. "The Social Scientist as Author: Clifford Geertz on Ethnography and Social Construction." *Journal of Advanced Composition* 11: 245–268, 1991.

Goldberg, Natalie. *Writing Down the Bones*. Boston: Shambhala, 1986.

Graves, Robert, and Alan Hodge. *The Reader Over Your Shoulder: A Handbook for Writers of English Prose*. New York: Vintage Books, 1979.

Holkeboer, Robert. *Creative Agony: Why Writers Suffer*. Bristol, Ind.: Wyndham Hall Press, 1986.

Howarth, William L. *The John McPhee Reader*. New York: Vintage Books, 1977.

Irving, John. "Getting Started." In *Writers on Writing*. Ed. Robert Pack and Jay Parini. Hanover, N.H.: Middlebury College Press, pp. 98–104.

Lamont, Anne. *Bird by Bird: Some Instructions on Writing and Life*. New York: Pantheon, 1994.

Latour, Bruno, and Steve Woolgar. *Laboratory Life: The Construction of Scientific Facts*. Princeton, N.J.: Princeton University Press, 1986.

Leader, Zachary. *Writer's Block*. Baltimore: Johns Hopkins University Press. 1991.

Myers, Greg. *Writing Biology: Texts in the Social Construction of Scientific Knowledge*. Madison: University of Wisconsin Press, 1990.

Mundis, Jerrold. *Break Writer's Block Now!* New York: St. Martins Press, 1991.

Murray, Donald M. "Teach Writing as a Process Not Product." *The Leaflet*, November 1972, pp. 11–14.

———. "Internal Revision: A Process of Discovery." In *Research on Composing: Points of Departure*. Ed. C. R. Cooper and L. Odell. Urbana, Ill.: NCTE, 1978, pp. 85–103.

———. "The Essential Delay: When Writer's Block Isn't." In *When a Writer Can't Write*. Ed. Mike Rose. New York: Guilford Press, 1985, pp. 219–226.

Nebel, Cecile. *The Dark Side of Creativity: Blocks, Unfinished Works and the Urge to Destroy*. Troy, N.Y.: Whitston Publishing Company, 1988.

Nelson, Victoria. *On Writer's Block*. Boston: Houghton Mifflin Company, 1993.

Olsen, Tillie. *Silences*. New York: Delacorte Press, 1978.

Ong, Walter. *Orality and Literacy: The Technologizing of the Word*. London: Methuen, 1982.

Parker, Dorothy. Interview. In *Writers at Work:* The Paris Review *Interviews*. First Series. Ed. Malcolm Cowley. New York: Viking, 1958, pp. 69–82.

Perl, Sondra. "Understanding Composing." *College Composition and Communication* 31: 363–369, 1980.

Richards, Pamela. "Risk." In *Writing for Social Scientists*. Ed. Howard Becker. Chicago: University of Chicago Press, 1986.

Rico, Gabriele Lusser. *Writing the Natural Way: Using Right-Brain Techniques to Release Your Expressive Powers*. Los Angeles: J. P. Tarcher, Inc., 1983.

Rose, Mike. "Rigid Rules, Inflexible Plans, and the Stifling of Language: A Cognitivist Analysis of Writer's Block." *College Composition and Communication* 31:389–401, 1980.

———. *Writer's Block: The Cognitive Dimension*. Carbondale: Southern Illinois University Press, 1984.

Rudestam, Kjell Erik, and Rae R. Newton. *Surviving Your Dissertation: A Comprehensive Guide to Content and Process*. Newbury Park, Calif.: Sage Publications, 1992.

Simenon, Georges. Interview. In *Writers at Work:* The Paris Review *Interviews*. First Series. Ed. Malcolm Cowley. New York: Viking, 1958, pp. 143–160.

Sommers, Nancy. "Revision Strategies of Student Writers and Adult Experienced Writers." *College Composition and Communication* 31: 378–388, 1980.

Stafford, Kim. "My Father's Place." *Hungry Mind Review* 28: 21, 1993–1994.

Stafford, William. *Writing the Australian Crawl: Views on the Writer's Vocation*. Ann Arbor: University of Michigan Press, 1978.

———. *You Must Revise Your Life*. Ann Arbor: University of Michigan Press, 1986.

Steinbeck, John. *Working Days: The Journals of* The Grapes of Wrath. Ed. Robert Demott. New York: Viking, 1989.

Tingle, Nick. "Peter and the Monolith: A Psychoanalytic Study of a Case of Writer's Block." *Journal of Advanced Composition* 8: 293–308, 1998.

Turner, Victor. *The Ritual Process: Structure and Anti-Structure*. Chicago: Aldine Publishing Company, 1969.

Ueland, Brenda. *If You Want to Write*. St. Paul, Minn.: Graywolf Press, 1987.

Van Gennep, Arnold. *The Rites of Passage*. Chicago: University of Chicago Press, 1960.

Welty, Eudora. *One Writer's Beginnings*. Cambridge, Mass.: Warner Books, 1983.

Woolf, Virginia. *A Room of One's Own*. San Diego: Harcourt Brace & Company, 1977.

———. *A Writer's Diary*. New York: Harcourt Brace Jovanovich, 1973.

Index